HUT! HUT! HIKE!

A HISTORY OF FOOTBALL TERMINOLOGY

TIMOTHY P. BROWN

BROWN HOUSE PUBLISHING

First printing 2022

ISBN: 978-0-9995723-6-8 (eBook)

ISBN: 978-0-9995723-7-5 (Paperback)

Brown House Publishing, Waterford, MI

✿ Created with Vellum

To Conor, Phil, MJ, Matt, and Javi,

for all the joy you give us.

CONTENTS

ACKNOWLEDGMENTS

Acknowledging those who helped make a book reality seldom captures their full contribution, but I'll give it a shot anyway, knowing these words fall short.

My deepest thanks go to my immediate family for supporting me while writing this book and listening to me ramble on about some little-known fact from football's past. Carolyn has borne the brunt of this burden, for which I am forever grateful. In addition, Conor, Phil, MJ, Javi, and Matt have contributed in their own ways. Phil's most important contribution was suggesting the book's title, while MJ created the original formation and play diagrams spread throughout.

They and others acted as sounding boards during the research and writing. Among the best steps I took was soliciting input from others on the terminology to include in this book. Larry Rosinski, Jim Mulcrone, Steve Brown, and Pat Brown each suggested many terms, with most suggestions making the final cut.

Besides providing input on terminology, Larry, Jim, and Phil gave feedback during the writing process that helped shape and improve the final product. In addition, Darin Hayes, who allows me to appear on his *Pigskin Dispatch* podcast each week, provided a thoughtful book review and spurred me to research one of my favorite origin stories, *The Granddaddy of Them All*.

Stewart Williams contributed excellent cover artwork for *How Football Became Football*, and equaled himself with this cover.

Thanks also to the archivists at libraries and other institutions who approved my use of their images in this book. More important, however, is to thank them for the many hours spent organizing and making their collections accessible to others.

I also thank Miriam Kleiman, Richard Schneider, and Ron Pomfrey for reminding me and others that football history can shed light on the role of sports in helping disparate elements of society gain shared experiences and understanding.

Thanks again to all!

PREFACE

The English language has more than 170,000 words in active use today, while another 40,000 have become obsolete. Languages are like that. Words come and go, though some seemingly live forever. This word churn occurs with ordinary, everyday words and in specific fields of study, industries, and games such as football. Football's word churn is driven by ever-changing rules, technological advances, coaching innovations, and broader social influences. Each alters the game, creating the need for new words to describe whatever's new.

Before leaking to the broader audience, most new football words begin as technical jargon used by players, coaches, and other insiders. Some terms, like "hut," are nonsensical, while others, like "hike," have a meaning beyond their use in football.

Sportswriters and other media figures are vital in spreading the jargon to the broader community. For instance, when a new coach comes to town or an old coach devises a new strategy, reporters learn the new terms and insert them in their writing to offer insight into the changes fans might notice. When publishing new terms, writers often place quotes around them or employ other writing devices to signify newness. For example, an early 1960s article might have quotes around "nickel coverage" or refer to "so-called dime coverage." In short order, however, writers stop defining such words as they become mainstream and understood by the average fan.

Because the evolution of football has been accompanied by a stream of new words, understanding when and why new terms arrived helps us understand the game's history. So, *Hut! Hut! Hike!* examines the history of football by identifying when standard football terms and expressions came into use and, when possible, explaining why the gridiron world needed those words.

With that goal in mind and focusing on football terminology understood by the public, this book relies heavily on information published in public sources, primarily newspapers. For much of football's history, newspapers and select magazines were the primary media through which the general or sporting public learned about football. Radio and television became critical media when they came along. Still, it is reasonable to assume that new football expressions appeared in different media at similar times. Since the print medium left the best record since football began, newspapers are the archive of choice.

The bulk of the research for this book occurred using an online newspaper archive -specifically newspapers.com- so must offer a few caveats. First, newspapers.com does not include every English, American, or Canadian newspaper or every issue of the newspapers it includes. Nevertheless, it is a comprehensive source with nearly 800 million newspaper pages as of November 2022.

Second, keyword searches perform splendidly at finding the entered terms but do not locate synonyms of those words, which can be problematic when football terminology changes over time. For example, a search for "blocking sled" would suggest that this barbarous tool first appeared in the 1930s since the term first showed up in newspapers during that decade. However, earlier versions of similar gadgets called charging machines or blocking machines were on football fields in the late 1890s. Same thing, different name. As such, there likely are earlier versions of some items described in this book, though I believe they are limited and went by another name anyway.

Third, the origins of terms with multiple meanings outside of football (e.g., pass, tackle) and multi-word expressions are more difficult to isolate than terms unique to football (e.g., crackback block). Tracing the origin of the crackback block was quick work, while other terms required extensive searches and the review of hundreds of articles. Some could not be isolated using the tools I chose.

For all those reasons, I undoubtedly missed earlier instances of some expressions. But, like a paleontologist whose interpretation and understanding of dinosaurs is based on the fossils uncovered to date, others will find stories I did not locate. Good for them, and I hope they let us know what they find. Feel free to contact me at my website, https://www.foot ballarchaeology.com/.

A final caveat is that the first person quoted using a term or expression is not necessarily the originator. The term might have bounced around for a few years before an enterprising reporter published it.

With all that said, I believe I have accurately portrayed when and why the overwhelming majority of the listed terms entered football.

INTRODUCTION

Before discussing the details of how various terms and expressions entered football, it is worth taking a quick spin through 150 years of football history to set the stage for the remainder of the book. This history will provide only broad brushstrokes over several pages.

Football historians commonly cite the Rutgers-Princeton contests of 1869 as the first football games, but those games resembled soccer matches more than rugby or the gridiron game that followed. Most intercollegiate games were soccer matches until students from several universities met in 1876 to form the Intercollegiate Football Association (IFA). The IFA members agreed to play by a consistent set of rules, copying rugby's sixty-one rules almost word-for-word. So, while it is often said that football evolved from rugby, it should be emphasized that early American football <u>was</u> rugby.

Some early football players, particularly Walter Camp and others at Yale, wanted a more controlled, "scientific" game than available played under rugby rules. Their leadership led the IFA to make several significant rule changes in the early 1880s that started the game down a path different from rugby. One change was to institute the concept of possession. Unlike a rugby scrum in which either team could gain possession of the ball, a new rule in 1880 allowed teams to keep possession of the ball from one scrimmage to the next. Unfortunately, the rule did not set conditions requiring teams to give up the ball, which led to problems in some games, so an 1882 modification required teams to gain five yards in three downs or forfeit possession. The play started from a scrimmage with a player on the side possessing the ball snapping it -with his feet- to a teammate (like a rugby scrum). Also, like rugby, runners had to be tackled between the waist and shoulders, making it challenging to bring ball carriers to the ground.

Another fundamental change from rugby began in 1884 when teammates began running alongside the ball carrier to ward off tacklers. These inter-ferers or blockers then began running in advance of the ball carrier, violating rugby's offside rule that players closer to the opponent's goal line than the ball could not engage in the play. While blocking became accepted, play remained rugby-like until an 1888 rule change allowed tackling below the waist, setting off another series of changes. With ball carriers more easily tackled, teams struggled to move the ball via the sweeping game, so they looked inward, shifting to a power game with plays run between the ends.

Offenses typically aligned in the Traditional T formation, but the rules did not require a minimum number of players on the line or limit player movement at the snap. Teams also used guards or tackles back formations that facilitated mass and momentum play, with multiple offensive players in motion at the snap, crashing into the line in advance of the runner. Teammates pushed the ball carrier from behind, pulled him, and occa-sionally threw him forward. Numerous injuries and some fatalities resulted, leading players to begin padding themselves. Despite some rule adjustments in the 1890s and early 1900s, the changes did not adequately reduce the game's dangers, so football came under pressure for funda-mental changes.

The pressure peaked in 1905. Teddy Roosevelt famously urged Harvard, Princeton, and Yale to lead this effort, but they proved unwilling. The November 1905 death of an NYU player led their university president to call a meeting of schools looking to reform football. That effort snow-balled, ultimately bringing numerous rule changes for the 1906 season, including legalizing the forward pass. Other 1906 rule changes required seven offensive players on the line of scrimmage, limited men in motion, and introduced the neutral zone and forward progress. The new rules also required teams to gain ten yards in three downs to encourage more open play. Numerous other rule changes occurred over the next five years, including the 1912 change giving offenses four downs to gain ten yards.

Initially, the forward pass had limited impact because teams lacked the techniques and concepts to take advantage of its possibilities. In addition, the early forward pass was heavily restricted by rule. Variously, incomplete passes resulted in turnovers, the ball could not be thrown more than twenty yards downfield or over the goal line, and the ball had to be thrown from at least five yards left or right of the center. However, despite the many restrictions that came and went until after WWII, the legal forward pass helped open up the game and was among the most important rule changes in the game's history.

Until 1912, the player receiving the snap from the center could not cross the line of scrimmage with the ball until he was five yards left or right of the center. Eliminating this rule expanded the options available to teams running the Notre Dame Box formation and the Single Wing, both of which were closed formations with all eleven players aligning near one another. Still, the game's popularity boomed, and the 1920s saw massive stadiums rise across the country while professional football began competing with the colleges for attention.

A second football revolution began immediately before and after WWII. Plastic helmets, face masks, and other equipment better protected the players, while two-platoon football entered the game, ultimately leading to the extreme specialization of today. The Modern T and Split T formations brought more sophisticated downfield passing and option football to the game. The T formation sent halfbacks in motion wide, then placed them wide as flankers or slots with one or both ends split, creating passing-oriented formations and offenses. In reaction, the most significant evolution in defenses occurred in the 1950s. Defenses addressed the offensive changes by abandoning six and seven-man fronts, moving players off the line and into linebacking and secondary roles. Defenses became the aggressor with blitzes and stunts. These changes helped redefine defenses, resulting in new defensive positions emerging in the 1950s and 1960s, many of whose names we use today.

Triple-option football emerged in the 1960s with the veer and wishbone. Football's long dalliance with spread offenses bore fruit in the 1970s and

1980s as one-back, and empty formations helped football become a passing game rather than a running game. The game has since witnessed the convergence of option and passing football with the zone read offense and RPO games.

	Early (1869-1905)	Middle (1906-1960)	Modern (1960+)
Leading Teams	Yale and Princeton	Big Ten	NFL
Offense	Traditional T and Guards Back	Single Wing, Modern T, or Split T	Modern T, Veer/Bone, or Spread
Defensive Linemen	Eight or Nine	Five to Seven	Three to Five
Headgear	None or leather harnesses	Leather helmet	Plastic helmet w/ face masks
Pads	None or stuffed	Molded leather / fiber	Plastic
Uniforms	Wool and cotton	Cotton and synthetic	Synthetic
Stadiums	Wood bleachers	Concrete bowl	Dome
Primary Medium	Newspaper	Radio	Television
# Officials	Three	Five	Six to Eight
# Coaches	Zero to Two	Four to Seven	Ten to Twenty
Top Game	IFA Thanksgiving	Rose Bowl	Super Bowl
Specialization	60-minute men	Limited specialization	Extreme specialization
Black Players	Isolated	Isolated	Dominant

A comparison of key elements of football across eras.

Off-The-Field Changes

Most terminology covered in this book concerns football as played on the field, but there is more to football than the game itself, and football's off-the-field elements have also seen tremendous change over the years. The game originated among elite Eastern colleges, became dominated by large state universities, and is now driven by professional football and the highly commercialized college game.

Segregated Native American colleges played the elite Eastern schools, but historically-black colleges and universities did not. A handful of Black players participated in early college and pro football. Still, they were banned from the pro game and largely excluded from college and pro football until the 1960s, yet they dominate both games today, at least in terms of the number of players.

Early college football teams were clubs whose admission fees paid for uniforms and travel. The game's increasing popularity led to big games being played at polo grounds and baseball stadiums. However, most occurred on open fields or small stadiums with wooden bleachers until after WWI. Opened in 1903, Harvard Stadium started the trend toward large stadiums holding tens of thousands while literally setting the field's dimensions in concrete. A post-war boom of memorial stadiums led to an increasingly commercialized game, as did the pro leagues that shifted from industrial towns to big cities, most of which lacked a dominant college football presence.

Newspapers helped popularize college football, and the development of sports pages covering football helped sell newspapers. Syndicated articles gave fans in rural Kansas familiarity with Harvard and Yale's stars, though few saw them in action, even in film clips. Commercial radio emerged in the 1920s, with some national broadcasts coming along in the 1930s and local television exploded after WWII. Still, television did not begin revolutionizing football until technological advances, and the *Sports Broadcasting Act of 1961* allowed the professional leagues to negotiate collective high-dollar contracts. Though late to the game, the colleges did the same, filling the pockets of coaches, players, and owners (or athletic departments). Finally, just as commercial radio allowed fans to hear games in real-time, television allowed them to see games live, in highlights, or on demand.

Commercialization and coaching interacted with one another throughout the game's history. Football began with team captains making personnel decisions, running practices, and leading teams during games. Coaches were recent graduates who volunteered their expertise and, by rule, could not actively coach during games. But the game became too important to be left in the hands of undergrads, so football coaching became a profession, first part-time and then full-time. Increased resources allowed teams to hire more coaches, while two-platoon football brought more specialized coaches and players. The sixty-minute man disappeared with college and pro rosters spots ultimately allocated to specialists, even down to micro-roles such as long snappers.

The language of football evolved with all these changes. Football began speaking the language of rugby, morphed into a dialect, and became a separate language when football and rugby players no longer understood one another. Though the two languages share many words, such as "onside," most no longer have a shared meaning. The coming pages will explain how, when, and why football's terminology or language evolved.

A few additional notes for the reader:

- This book is organized by decade and term or set of terms within a decade. Each story stands alone so readers can leaf through the book, picking and choosing items of interest. Still, some explanations presuppose knowledge covered earlier in the book.
- The Bibliography and Index are organized alphabetically and include the starting page number for each term.

1

IN THE BEGINNING

Football, Rugby, Soccer, and Varsity

Across the world and back in ancient times, men competed in games that involved kicking, batting, or throwing a ball into their opponent's goal. Our gridiron game descends most directly from English folk contests where young men competed by kicking an inflated pig's bladder into the neighboring village. They played the games as the weather turned chilly because the post-harvest pig slaughter supplied the kickable bladders.

The kicking game became known as **football**, but its rules varied until a few chaps in London created the *Football Association* in 1863 to establish consistent rules. The Association rules did not allow players to touch the ball with their hands or arms, while a similar game played at *The Rugby School* in Warwickshire allowed players to pick up and run with the ball. This game became known as **rugby**.

FOOT BALL, KINGSTON-UPON-THAMES,
SHROVE TUESDAY, FEB. 24TH 1846.

An illustration of foot ball played at Kingston-upon-Thames on
Shrove 1846. (Public domain)

The zany students at the University of Oxford in the 1880s created slang terms by adding -er to the end of certain words. Rugby became "rugger," and the Association game became "asoccer," before being shortened to **soccer**. The Brits, and citizens of other foolish nations, continued calling the hands-free game football and the hands-on game rugby. Likewise, crew teams at American colleges borrowed a slang term from their British counterparts who had dropped the first two syllables of "university" to produce 'varsity, and, eventually, **varsity**, a term that transferred to football in the early 1890s.

After the Civil War, American college students started playing the Association game. Harvard switched to rugby after their pals from McGill University in Montreal showed them the hands-on game. A few years later, students from several Northeastern colleges formed the *Intercollegiate Football Association* and adopted a slightly-modified form of rugby as their rules. The compounding effect of their tweaking the rules year after year gave us today's football game.

For much of the 1880s, Americans called all three games football or used adjectives to distinguish Association football, rugby football, and gridiron football, with the latter appearing in print by 1891. As gridiron football became dominant in the United States, Americans called it football, while the Association game became soccer.

Our friends to the north played soccer and traditional English rugby in addition to a game known as Canadian rugby, with elements of rugby and gridiron football. Canadian rugby became the primary fall sport up there and shifted its rules toward the gridiron game over many decades, leading their national associations to update their names. *The Interprovincial Rugby Football Union* and the *Western Interprovincial Rugby Football Union* merged in 1958 to form the *Canadian Football League*. Likewise, the amateur *Canadian Rugby Union* became the *Canadian Amateur Football Association* in 1966.

Pigskin

The balls used in the early kicking games were inflated pig bladders, while Association balls of the 1860s and 1870s were bladders wrapped in pigskin. However, the use of pigskin as a nickname for the round ball never caught on in England, perhaps because pigskin was already a common term for polo and steeplechase saddles. Although Americans sometimes wrote of saddled horsemen being "in the pigskin," football adopted **pigskin** as a nickname for the ball and the game more broadly by the mid-1880s.

Early footballs varied in size, generally taking the shape of a plum. Richard Linton, a cobbler in Rugby, England, was the first to substitute a rubber bladder for the pig bladder in the mid-1850s. He also standardized the manufacturing process, which resulted in the balls he produced being nearly round.

Linton's round ball proved popular among Association football players. Still, he continued producing an oval ball preferred by rugby players, which became the standard size and shape for rugby balls moving forward.

Goal, Goal Line, Goal Posts, Uprights, and Crossbar

The term **goal** comes from the old English word "gol," meaning boundary. As the English folk games formalized, teams marked boundary lines or **goal lines** at either end of the playing area and competed by kicking the ball across the opponent's lines. Later, they placed two posts on the goal line with a rope or bar between them. Most people playing these games in England scored points by kicking the ball under the bar, as reflected in today's Association or soccer rules. Besides allowing players to pick up and run with the ball, the students at *The Rugby School* also chose to score points by kicking the ball over the crossbar. This approach became embedded in the game of rugby.

An 1868 depiction of English rugby includes a goal post.
(Godefroy Durand, Public domain)

Many related football terms came over from rugby. For example, "goal post" appears in the 1860 coverage of an Australian rugby match, while upright and cross-bar appear in an 1870 English article about rugby's rules.

> The goals are upright posts of indefinite height -from 15 to 16 feet being perhaps the best, with a cross-bar 10 feet from the ground joining them, over which the ball must be kicked to score a goal.[1]

Likewise, upright and cross-bar are part of Rule 4 from the IFA's 1876 rules.

Rule 4: Each goal shall be composed of two upright posts exceeding 11 feet in height from the ground and placed 18 feet 6 inches apart, with a cross-bar 10 feet from the ground.[2]

Americans used all three terms during football's formative years. **Goal posts** premiered in an 1875 article about the first Harvard-Yale game, mentioning that a kick went through the goal posts but failed to count because it hit the rope functioning as the crossbar. **Crossbar** first appeared in 1877 in a report on the Harvard-Princeton game. Finally, while the various rugby and football rules describe the posts as being upright, the first use of **uprights** as a slang noun came in an 1890 article about the Chicago-Penn game.

Touch Line, Out of Bounds, and Sideline

The early terms describing the field differed from today. For example, the borders running the field's length were the **touchlines**, and the areas outside the lines were **in touch**. The touchlines were boundary lines, so they were also known as *bound lines*, and the area outside the bound lines was **out of bounds**. Touchline fell out of use in the 1890s as the game adopted **sideline** as the preferred term.

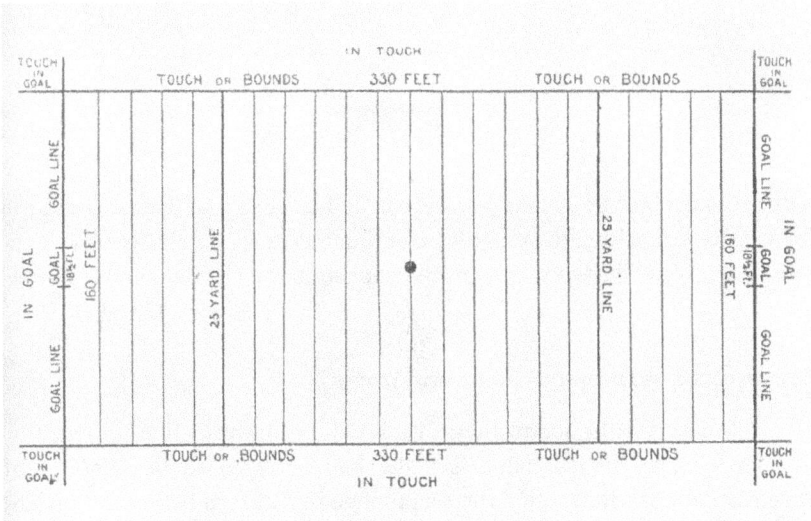

The terminology used to describe the football field was transitioning when Stagg and Williams published their 1893 book. (Stagg and Williams, 1893).

Yard Line and Gridiron

Football fields initially had the same markings as rugby fields with only five stripes: two goal lines, two sidelines, and a midfield line. However, with the introduction of the "system of downs" in 1882, teams had to gain five yards in three downs or lose possession of the ball. To help game officials monitor the yards gained, Walter Camp suggested adding stripes or **yard lines** every five yards, leading a fellow committee member to say, "The field will look like a **gridiron**." (A gridiron is a frame of parallel bars or beams set at right angles to other bars or beams.) The term "gridiron" has been tied to football ever since.

Field Dimensions and Markings (1882-1902)

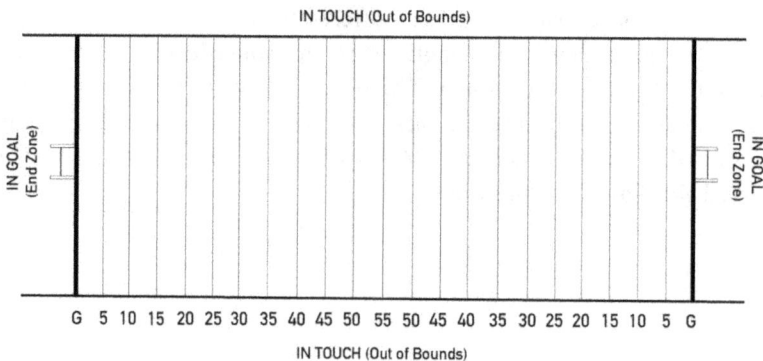

IN TOUCH (Out of Bounds)

IN GOAL (End Zone)

IN GOAL (End Zone)

G 5 10 15 20 25 30 35 40 45 50 55 50 45 40 35 30 25 20 15 10 5 G

IN TOUCH (Out of Bounds)

The areas beyond the goal lines were called **in goal,** and the field did not have a stripe marking the end of the in touch area. The field also had a **55-yard line.** We will discuss how both changed in the chapter on the 1910s.

Scrummage, Scrimmage, Snap, and Down

In a rugby **scrum** or **scrummage**, each team's forwards line up, pushing and shoving as an official tosses the ball between them. (The rugby scrummage was often called the scrimmage in America before 1880.) The forwards then attempt to kick the ball to teammates standing behind the respective lines. Walter Camp and others viewed the scrum as a game of chance because each team could gain possession. Wanting teams to have greater control of their destinies, Camp convinced the rules committee to approve the **scrimmage** in 1880. By starting play from a controlled scrimmage with one team maintaining possession of the ball for several downs, football shifted to structured play, different from the free-flowing nature of soccer and rugby. The team possessing the ball started each play from scrimmage when one of their rushers or linemen placed his foot on the ball and rolled it back to another player. This procedure became known as a **snap** back.

Finally, because the American gridiron rules were nearly identical to England's rugby rules, a play ended when an opponent tackled the ball carrier and held him to the ground until the ball carrier yelled, "Down." When football shifted to the scrimmage in 1880, each play from scrimmage became known as a **down**.

Referee and Umpire

When the IFA laid down its original rules, the rules concerning the officials were among the few rugby rules the collegians modified. England's rugby rules assumed opposing team captains could honorably handle disputes. American footballers knew better and opted for an impartial referee and two umpires appointed by and representing the teams. The umpires, sometimes called *judges*, ruled on scoring and out of bounds, while advocating for their teams in disputes. The arrangement proved unsatisfactory, and in 1883, they switched to two impartial officials: a referee and an umpire.

The referee was responsible for the ball. He judged where to place the ball, ruled on out-of-bounds issues, and determined whether the ball crossed the goal line or passed through the uprights. The umpire controlled the players, monitoring fouls and unfair tactics. Both kept busy, particularly the umpire who had to monitor twenty-two players capable of foul play.

Onside, Offside, and Blocking

Football involves two teams or sides attempting to move the ball toward their goal and away from the other side's goal. Originally, a player behind or closer to his team's goal than a teammate possessing the ball was considered **onside**. Conversely, a player nearer the opponent's goal than the teammate with the ball was **offside,** and the rules prohibited offside players from participating in the action.

The offside rule kept teammates from running ahead of the ball carrier to interfere with or block an opponent. However, in 1884, a team or two had players run alongside the ball carrier to ward off potential tacklers. Although it was illegal, the warders began running ahead of the ball carrier to ward off opponents. The practice became accepted, enshrined in the rules, and became known as interference or **blocking**.

Similarly, while it was legal before 1906 for players to toss or hand the ball to teammates who were onside -they referred to all methods of transferring the ball as passing- giving the ball to a teammate who was ahead of the ball or offside remained illegal. Legalizing the forward pass in 1906 violated the offside rule central to rugby, but the rule makers opted to make that change anyway.

While the technicalities differ from the old days, the core principle underlying today's offside penalty remains a player being on the wrong side of the ball at the snap.

Fumble, Scoop-and-Score, and Muff

The 1880 shift to the rule of possession resulted in the need for a term to describe instances when a player accidentally lost control of the ball by, for instance, dropping it. Baseball writers of the era sometimes referred to errors as **fumbles**, so football borrowed the term. The first documented mention of a fumble in a football game came during an 1893 Princeton victory over when Lafayette's center fumbled. Princeton's Tracy Harris scooped up the ball, running the field's length for a touchdown. Thus, the first documented fumble was also the first known **scoop-and-score**, a term that did not appear for another 113 years, when it showed up at the University of Miami in 1996 and a week later at Marine City High School in Michigan.

FOOTBALL, 1885.
R. M. Hodge, '86. H. P. Toler, '86. C. M. DeCamp, '86. H. W. Cowan, '88. H. C. Lamar, '88. H. L. Hodge, '86. J. C. Adams, '88.
T. H. Harris, '86.   W. J. Cook, '86.   H. S. Savage, '87.
C. E. Griffith, '86.   W. M. Irvine, '88.   H. W. Ford, '89.

Tracy Harris (second from the left), the first player known to
recover a fumble, with Princeton's 1885 football team. (Presbrey
and Moffatt, 1901)

"Fumble" entered the conversation in the early 1880s but did not appear
in football's rules until 1899. Similarly, football borrowed its companion
term, **muff**, from baseball by 1895, joining fumble in the 1899 rule book.
(A fumble requires a player to possess the ball, a muff does not require
possession, only contact.)

Tackle, Maul, Maul-In Goal, Touchdown, Forward Progress, In The Grasp, and Down by Contact

Tackle comes from Old English and relates to a ship's rigging and cargo
handling. Horse tack, thumb tack, block-and-tackle, and the sporting
sense of tackle share a common ancestor. Football's "tackle" appeared in
the game's first set of rules, including:

> Rule 10: A tackle is made when the holder of the ball is held by one or
> more players of the opposite side.

> Rule 18: In the event of any player holding or running with the ball being
> tackled, and the ball fairly held, he must at once cry down, and there put it
> down.[3]

A TACKLE.

An illustration of a runner tossing the ball to a teammate while being tackled. ('A College Game,' *Albany Ledger*, May 6, 1887.)

Like rugby today, runners in early football often stayed on their feet while being tackled, so their teammates bound to them, pushing and pulling them toward the goal line while the defense pushed in the opposite direction. These packs of players pushing and pulling were called **mauls**. Mauls could lead to the offense gaining or losing ground because the concept of forward progress was not yet part of the game.

Mauls sometimes started near a goal line and crossed it, entering the "in goal" area. This particular type of maul was a "maul in goal" or **maul-in**, which had three potential outcomes. The maul-in could be pushed back onto the field of play, a defender could take the ball from the ball carrier, or the ball carrier could touch the ball to the ground in goal to achieve a **touchdown.**

Early American football and English rugby were nearly identical, so this 1882 illustration of an English rugby maul-in reflects how an American football maul-in might have looked. (*Supplement to the Illustrated London News,* January 14, 1882)

The IFA eliminated the need to touch the ball down in goal in 1885, instead awarding the touchdown when the ball crossed the goal line in an offensive player's possession. Eliminating the need to touch the ball down was the first step toward football recognizing **forward progress**. However, while the rule eliminated maul-in goals, the ball carrier still had to be brought to the ground and held when tackled between the goal lines.

After the idea floated around for more than a decade, a 1905 rule applied forward progress to the entire field. Then, in 1906, runners were down when any part of their body other than their hands and feet touched the ground, the runner was in an opponent's grasp, or the runner's forward progress stopped.

The NCAA dropped the **in the grasp** portion of the rule in 1932, and the NFL did the same in 1956. However, the NFL still required the runner to be **down by contact**, not simply down, and that distinction remains in place today.

Finally, mauls made a comeback when the NFL legalized pushing or charging into a teammate carrying the ball in 2005, and the NCAA followed suit in 2013. (Pushing remains illegal in high school football.)

Rouge, Safety Touchdown, Safety, and Touchback

As rugby evolved in England, there were competing rules, some of which awarded the opponent a point when a team touched the ball down in their own goal, a procedure known as a minor or a **rouge**. When America's IFA created its rules in 1876, it used a version of rugby rules that did not include the rouge. However, some rugby-playing Canadians used rules allowing the rouge, and it made its way into the Canadian game.

Early American football did not include the rouge. Teams with the ball deep in their territory could touch it down in their own goal, take the ball to the 25-yard line, and either retain possession or dropkick to the other team. Teams touching the ball down in their own goal played it safe, and the tactic was known as a *safety touchdown*, also called a **safety**.

As might be imagined, some teams used the safety touchdown so often that it hindered the spirit of the game (see the Yale-Princeton block games of 1880 and 1881), leading to a rule change. Under the new rule, a team causing the ball to go behind their goal line and touching the ball down in goal committed a safety, earning the opposing team one point. The opposing team began receiving two points per safety starting in 1884.

The same rule determined that if the opposing team had caused the ball to go behind the goal line before it was touched down, it became a "touch in goal" or **touch-back**. Teams taking a touchback could scrimmage or kick from the 25-yard line. They opponent did not receive points.

Drop Kick, Place Kick, Punt, Goal from Field, Field Goal, Placer, and Holder

Football's first three rules defined three kicks:

> Rule 1: A **drop kick**, or drop, is made by letting the ball fall from the hands and kicking it the very instant it rises.

> Rule 2: A **place kick**, or place, is made by kicking the ball after it has been placed in a nick made in the ground for the purpose of keeping it at rest.

> Rule 3: A **punt** is made by letting the ball fall from the hands and kicking it before it hits the ground.[4]

Originally, there were two ways to score goals. The first was the **goal from field**, a kick on a scrimmage play, which almost immediately became known as a **field goal**. As a scrimmage kick, the defense could contest the goal from field, which forced teams to attempt field goals via drop kicks.

The second way to score a goal came following a touchdown when teams gained the opportunity to kick a **goal from touchdown**, which was a free kick, meaning the defense faced restraints in trying to block the kick.

	Touchdown	Goal From Field	Try After Touchdown	Safety
1883	2	5	4	1
1884	2	5	4	2
1887	4	4	2	2
1898	5	5	1	2
1904	5	4	1	2
1909	4	3	1	2
1912	6	2	1	2
1958	6	3	1 or 2	2

Football changed from the touchdown-goal equivalency system to points-based scoring in 1883. It was not until 1898 that the goal or try after a touchdown was worth one point.

Before 1898, the rule book referred to the player who placed the ball on the ground as the **placer**. That person also became known as the **holder** by 1895. The switch nearly coincided with a technique invented in 1896. Instead of drop-kicking goals from the field, teams had the center snap to a teammate squatting or sitting several yards back, who placed or held the ball on the ground for the placekicker.

Quarterback, Fullback, Halfback, Snapper-back, Snap-back, Center, Guard, Tackle, End, Offensive Line, Running Back, Offense, and Defense

The amended Rugby Union game played from 1876 to 1879 included 15 players per side. Offenses often aligned in something resembling the Traditional T formation with ten rushers or forwards, now called linemen, and five backs.

The naming convention for the backs carried over from rugby and reflected their proximity to the scrum. The player aligned further back was the *goal-tend*, *back*, or **full-back**. Other players set half as deep as the fullback were **half-backs**. Finally, the quarter-back was the player who received the snap and aligned between the halfbacks and the forwards. The fifth back positioned himself between the halfbacks and fullback, so he was the *three-quarterback* or the third-in-hand.

The forwards were not distinguished by position until the mid-to-late 1880s. With the change from scrummage to scrimmage, the player snapping the ball became the "**snapper-back**" or "**snap-back**" by 1884. Since he was in the middle of the seven linemen, he was also called the **center**.

The remaining forwards received distinct position names by 1887. Since football did not have a neutral zone until 1905, the linemen on defense sometimes struck the center or the ball before the snap. The players aligned next to the center protected the center, and became known as **guards**.

Early offenses often ran plays just outside the guards, resulting in the defensive players across the line making many tackles, so they became **tackles**, a position named for its defensive role rather than offense role. And, of course, the players outside the tackles were the last ones on the line, so people called them **ends**.

Typically, the front wall of the offense was called forwards, while those on defense were rushers. The forwards were called the **offensive line** for the first time in 1893 in an article about Iowa preparing for its Thanksgiving game with Nebraska. That seems appropriate since both schools have produced their share of offensive linemen.

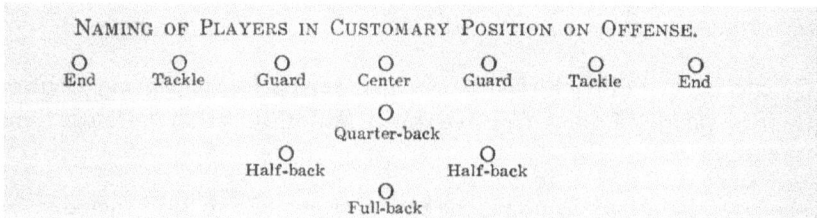

NAMING OF PLAYERS IN CUSTOMARY POSITION ON OFFENSE.

O	O	O	O	O	O	O
End	Tackle	Guard	Center	Guard	Tackle	End

O
Quarter-back

O		O
Half-back		Half-back

O
Full-back

The 1917 Official Foot Ball Rules diagram shows the fullback farthest from the center, the halfbacks somewhat closer, and the quarterback between the halfbacks and the center.

Around 1890, the quarterback, halfbacks, and fullback became known collectively as **running backs**. During the same period, the "attacking team," or, as the rule book described them, "the team which has the ball," became the **offense,** and the opponent became the **defense**.

T Formation

Although this book uses the term "Traditional T formation" to describe the most common offensive alignment used from the game's beginning until the turn of the century, the term was not used then. Instead, it was called the straight formation, the close formation (Walter Camp), or regular formation (Pop Warner) to distinguish it from the guards back, tackles back, and tandem formations that arose in the 1890s.

Nevertheless, the **T formation** was the era's standard, a label first used in 1903. It had seven linemen aligned near one another in a balanced set. The quarterback stood about one yard from the center, directly behind or to one side. The fullback set behind the center; the halfbacks aligned slightly in front of or even with the fullback.

Traditional T

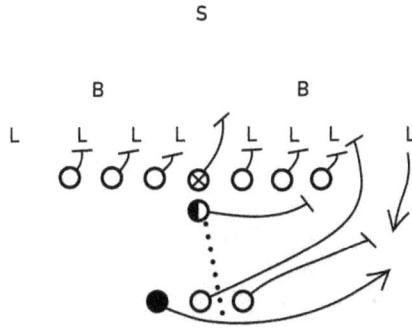

Illustration of a sweep from the Traditional T formation. The center snaps the ball to the quarterback, who laterals to the left halfback before joining the other backs blocking to the right.

Wedge, Flying Wedge, and Sweep

As described previously, teams began having players run alongside and in advance of the ball carrier in 1884. The same year, Princeton and Penn were locked in a scoreless tie when Richard Hodge, Princeton's quarterback, instructed his teammates to form a V around him and push forward at the snap of the ball. Penn did not have an answer for Princeton's V Trick as the Tigers won going away, 31-0. The tactic remained known as the V Trick until 1889, when it became the **wedge**, variations of which remain in football today.

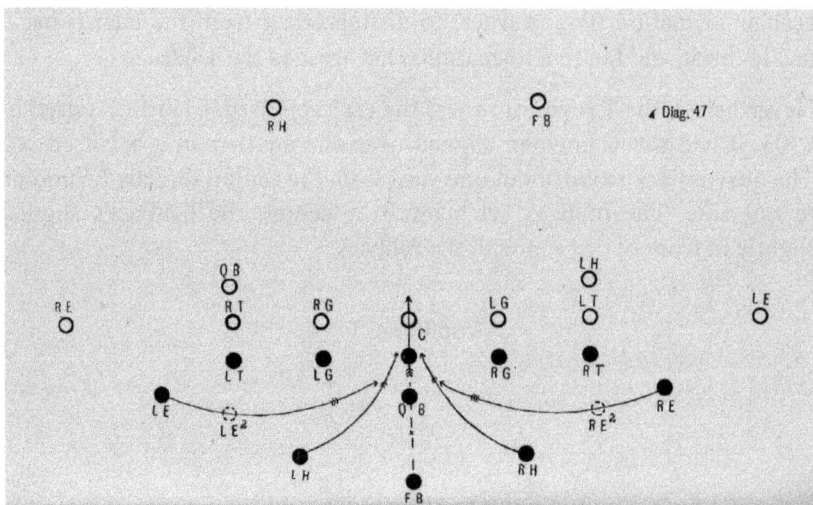

A diagram of Stagg and Williams' center wedge. (Stagg and Williams, 1893)

The wedge then came into use by the kicking team on kickoffs. Whereas the kicking team generally loses possession of the ball under today's rules, the kickoff in early football resembled the process seen in soccer today. Typically, the kicker dribbled or booted the ball a few inches, picked it up, and ran with it. After the wedge from scrimmage emerged, teams applied the idea to the kickoff by forming a V or wedge near the kicker and enveloping him once he kicked the ball.

Lorin F. Deland, a Harvard fan who created new plays as a hobby, modified that process in 1892 by having the kicker's teammates line up in a wedge formation ten yards behind the kicker and run forward shortly before he kicked the ball. The kicker dribbled and picked up the ball before slipping behind the **Flying Wedge**. However, since the play led to many injuries, it was outlawed in 1894.

Harvard's original Flying Wedge during their 1892 clash with Yale in Springfield, MA. (Davis, 1911)

Of course, teams did not always run the ball up the middle; they also ran plays over the guards, tackles, ends, and around the ends. Running around the end did not have a particular name until 1889 when **sweep** swept through the football world.

Coach, Head Coach, Assistant Coach, and Graduate Assistant Football Coach

American football began as a club sport among friends at various colleges and universities. These club teams elected captains who managed the rosters and practices and coordinated with the referee during games. More experienced players taught the new game to the rookies, as did alums who returned to practice for a few days each year to instruct and scrimmage with the current team.

By the late 1880s, however, the big rivalry games attracted thousands or tens of thousands of fans, so winning and losing could no longer be left in the hands of the team captain. Instead, Yale adopted a system where the previous year's captain remained on campus to manage the team the following year. In addition, schools with less football tradition and expertise hired former Yale, Princeton, and other Eastern players to instruct their teams on the latest techniques and strategies.

American sports then borrowed another British term to describe these instructors. As in America, the British used "coach" to describe horse-drawn vehicles that carried people from one place to another. University of Oxford students in the 1830s began using "coach" as slang for a tutor that carried a student through his classes. The term transferred over to sports instructors and then crossed the water. **Football coach** first appeared in an American newspaper in 1889, one year after "baseball coach" made its premiere. Those in coaching roles were sometimes called "coachers" early on.

George A. Stewart, Harvard class of 1884, was the first to be called a **head coach** when he accepted the captains' invitation to handle the 1893 Harvard team. **Assistant coach** appeared in Britain in 1889, while Harvard had an assistant coach for baseball in 1893. The first to be called an assistant coach in football was Brick Whitehouse. He played for Stanford in 1893 and assisted in preparing Stanford for the fourth playing of the Big Game with California in 1894. Whitehouse was called an assistant coach in articles detailing an altercation the night of Stanford's win over California when Whitehouse and a friend were shot in a San Francisco saloon. Both survived. The assailant pled guilty to two charges of assault with a deadly weapon and walked out of the court after paying a $1,000 fine.

THOMAS. LEADBETTER. WALTON. LEWIS. FRANKENHEIMER. HARRELSON. MAYNARD. POP BLISS. KENNEDY.
WILSON. WHITEHOUSE. BURNETT. CODE. DOWNING, P MCMILLAN. COCHRAN. DOWNING, C. HALL.

The 1893 Stanford football team includes Brick Whitehouse, sitting second from
the left, and coach Pop Bliss, standing second from the right in his Yale sweater.
(1894 Stanford *Quad*)

Besides the head and assistant coaches, football staffs received additional
support from volunteer coaches and recent graduates considering the
coaching business. The latter followed a role the academic departments at
American universities had filled since the 1870s or earlier, the graduate
assistant. Those in academic departments often received fellowships that
paid their tuition and a stipend. In the athletic department, the **graduate
assistant football coach** held a similar apprentice role ranging from
performing menial coaching tasks to on-the-field coaching, depending on
the individual and staff qualifications.

Trainer

Whether they dealt with horses, jockeys, or runners, **trainers** were
involved in the athletic world long before the first gridiron game. Athletic
clubs and university gymnasia hired trainers to work with members and
students. While their knowledge was pre-scientific, many respected
trainers for their ability to build stamina and prepare athletes for their
target sport. A handful also became known for developing knee braces
and other therapeutic equipment.

Mike Murphy was among the top early trainers at Yale, Michigan, and Penn. Some referred to him as the "Father of American track." (1909 University of Pennsylvania *Record*)

Early trainers typically were not involved in football techniques or play calling. Instead, they ensured the players' conditioning, mended aches and minor injuries, and advised or ran the training table. Hence, they combined today's strength and conditioning, medical or training, and nutrition staff duties. Trainers continued in their multi-disciplinary role until the 1920s, when the term became focused on those handling injury prevention and treatment.

Football Sweater, Varsity Sweater, Letter Sweater, Watch Charm, and Letter Jacket

The first sports team to wear a letter emblem on their uniform was Harvard's 1865 baseball team. The story goes that the team manager ordered sweaters bearing the letter H and awarded them to players for their play and work. Harvard's football team picked up the practice ten years later, allowing its starters to keep their sweater or jersey at the season's end. Thus began the tradition of awarding varsity letter sweaters and related items.

The 1865 Harvard baseball team was the first to wear a school
letter or logo on their uniform. (Public domain)

In the 1890s, the tradition evolved from players keeping their game-worn
sweaters to being awarded separate sweaters, often cardigans better
suited to social settings than the gridiron. The sweaters were known
as **football sweaters**, a generic term much like "football jersey" today, or
as **varsity sweaters** when the practice expanded to other sports. Some
schools created separate letter symbols for each sport, a practice that
would be frowned upon by the brand identity crowd today. **Letter
sweater** entered the conversation in 1903 to reflect the diversity of those
earning such awards.

The 1890s also saw schools award athletes with gold badges or **watch
charms** to hang on their pocket watch chains. For example, Trinity
College in Connecticut awarded gold badges to those football players
starting and playing the entirety of thirteen or more games during their
careers.

The 1893 football team wearing UNC's first athletic uniforms. (1894 University of North Carolina at Chapel Hill *Hellenium*)

A year later, Amos Alonzo Stagg created the "Order of the C" letter winners' club at Chicago, the first formal letter awarded by a school. Chicago's other innovation was to award blankets to its seniors to acknowledge long-term commitment and excellence. While many could earn a letter for their performance during a single season, blankets were reserved for those lettering in the same sport for three or four years.

The next great innovation in letter-related gear came in the 1930s with the arrival of the **letter jacket**. The earliest reports of letter jackets came from Trinity University in San Antonio. Letter jackets remained in Texas and Oklahoma for the next few years before exploding onto the national scene.

Box Seat, Box Office, and Press Box

There are competing stories for the origin of **box seats**. One suggests that carriage drivers often sat atop a box that provided a favorable view of the road ahead. Another story indicates the term arose from the practice of theater owners separating their front rows from the rest of the audience via rails or half walls. Elevated seating areas near the front of the theater were also called box seats. Stadiums with box seats were used for football games by the mid-1890s, as seen in the following image.

Some fans sat in the box seats when the Boston Athletic Club visited the Chicago Athletic Club. ('They Tie At Four,' *Chicago Tribune*, November 29, 1895.)

Advertisements for an 1811 circus in New York City mentioned box seats and as did an 1820 newspaper article concerning a Mississippi theater. Theatergoers could purchase spots in the preferred seating areas in advance from the **box office**. Box office appears in stories related to ticket sales and game attendance for college football by 1893.

As baseball and other sports stadium operators sought the coverage and publicity provided by newspapers and magazines in the late 1880s, they offered advantageous, separate seating to reporters. Such areas became known as the **press box,** with the first mentions of press boxes at football games coming at the 1892 Yale-Princeton game at Manhattan Field in New York and the 1893 Harvard-Yale game in Springfield, Massachusetts.

The boys in the press box monitored the Illini from their spot atop the Illinois Field bleachers, which stood twenty rows high. (1912 Illinois *Illio,* University of Illinois Archives)

Father of American Football

Although commonly attributed to an 1892 *Harper's Weekly* article by Caspar Whitney, Camp was first called the "Father of Football" in an 1886 article concerning the dispute over the winner of that year's Yale-Princeton game. By that point, Camp had played at Yale from 1876 to 1882 and remained an active advisor after that, but he did not "coach" Yale until 1888, two years after being called the "father of football."

Still, as one of Yale's representatives to the Intercollegiate Football Associations, Camp had been the chief proponent of critical rule changes that took football down a path different than rugby. In addition, Camp was called the "Father of American football" in 1890 and the "Father of the Gridiron Game" in 1895.

Walter Camp, the "Father of the Gridiron Game."
[*Mr. Camp will coach the Stanford Eleven for the great game with Berkeley on Thanksgiving Day.—Drawn from a photograph.*]

Walter Camp was first referred to as the Father of the Gridiron Game in the caption to this illustration. (*San Francisco Examiner*, October 10, 1895.)

Cheerleader

America's first **cheerleaders** performed at political rallies and parades to rile up the crowds. Princeton's locomotive cheer arrived at the station in the 1870s when stirring renditions of *"Hurrah! Hurrah! Tiger! S-s-s-t! Boom! A-h-h-h!"* filled the air. In addition, Princeton was the first to have the student body elect fellow students to lead organized yells and songs at football games in the 1890s.

The Tigers went so far as to organize separate cheer teams to yell during practice. One supported the varsity, and the other supported the scrubs or scout team.

All early cheerleaders were male because many colleges had all-male student bodies. However, in 1914, Kansas' Elizabeth Morrow became the first female cheerleader to raise her voice to the crowd.

Cleat. Since gridiron football began, players wore calf or kangaroo-skin shoes with leather **cleats**, like those used in English rugby and soccer.

Fair Catch. The **fair catch** came into football with the adoption of rugby's rules and gains a newspaper mention in 1878. While we think of the fair catch only in terms of kicking plays today, it applied to several non-kicking plays in football's early days.

Quick Kick. Teams in unfavorable field positions punted on early downs after football introduced the system of downs in 1882. The first use of **quick kick** in that context came in 1889.

First Half, Halftime, and Second Half. Football borrowed **first half**, **halftime**, and **second half** from rugby. Each saw use in the U.K. before 1876 and were included in descriptions of American football games in the 1870s.

Training Table. Beginning in the early 1880s, the Harvard crew team ate their meals together on a diet controlled by the captain and team advisors. Their football team adopted the same strategy while in training, so the meals were called **training table**.

2

THE EIGHTEEN NINETIES

Signals, Signal Drill, and Going Against Air

The transition from the scrummage to the scrimmage in 1880 led to football developing structured offensive plays, but that change did not occur overnight. Initially, the scrimmage was merely a controlled method of initiating action in a rugby-style game. Over several years, however, offenses recognized that coordinated effort was more effective than winging it. For example, teams covered punts on early downs more effectively when each member of the offense knew they were punting. Likewise, offensive linemen blocked better when they knew the ball would be run to the left or right.

This recognition led teams to develop structured plays called at the line of scrimmage via coded **signals**. Some team captains or quarterbacks used hand signals, such as placing their right hand on their hip or pulling up their left sock, but most used voice commands consisting of short phrases or sentences. For example, "Play up sharp, Charlie," "Play up, Charlie," or "Charlie" might indicate a punt, while other word combinations designated running plays. By the 1890s, teams named their plays using two-digit numbers, and while easier to communicate than short phrases, numbered plays still required players to memorize their responsibility for each play. This approach limited the playbook size, but in football's one-platoon days, the available practice time also limited the number of plays teams could memorize. Still, Stagg and Williams' 1893 book, *American*

Football, includes sixty-nine plays named by numbers, so players potentially had much to remember.

One method of teaching and honing plays was by lining up, the quarterback called the signals, and the team executed the play without opposition. A regular part of early football practices and pre-game warmups,
this process was known as **signal drills**.

Yale's quarterback prepares to receive the snap during signal drills
before their 1908 game at West Point. Yale won 6-0. (George
Grantham Bain Collection, Library of Congress)

Some still refer to running plays without opposition as signal drills,
though **going against air** emerged in the mid-1980s and is the popular
expression today.

Onside Kick and Roughing

Recall from the previous chapter that a player was onside by being behind
or closer to his team's goal than the teammate possessing the ball. A
player nearer to the opponent's goal than a teammate with the ball was
offside. Offside players could not participate in the action.

George Woodruff, who played at Yale from 1885 to 1888 and was a player-
coach at Penn from 1892 to 1895, recognized that the onside definition
presented an opportunity, which he exploited in 1893. Woodruff had his

quarterback take the snap and immediately punt it toward a sideline. The teammates behind the punter at the kick were considered onside and could run downfield to recover the punt. Teammates in front of the punter at the kick were offside but became onside and eligible to recover the ball if the quarterback (punter) passed them while running downfield. This tactic became known as an **onside kick** (from scrimmage) or quarterback kick.

An example onside kick came in Penn's 1893 game with Harvard:

> On Harvard's fifteen yard line, Pennsylvania tried a neat trick called an **onside kick.** Williams, the quarter back, kicked the ball [from] behind his rush line across the field, and Simmons, the end rusher, got it on Harvard's five yard line.[1]

The onside kick from scrimmage remained part of American football in various forms through the 1922 season and is legal in Canada today.

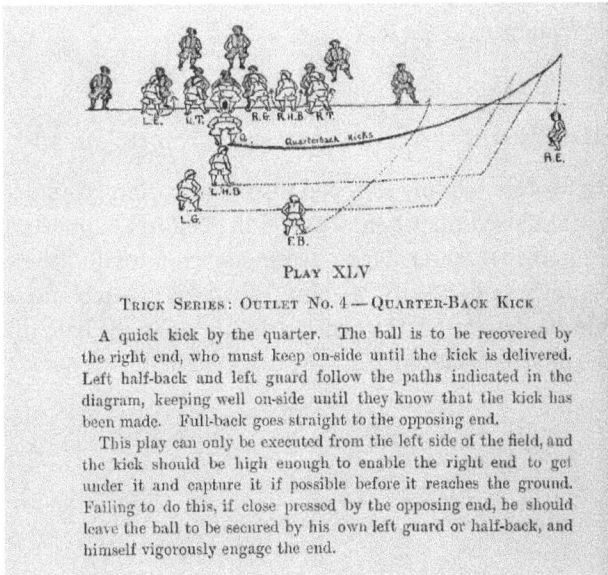

PLAY XLV

TRICK SERIES: OUTLET No. 4 — QUARTER-BACK KICK

A quick kick by the quarter. The ball is to be recovered by the right end, who must keep on-side until the kick is delivered. Left half-back and left guard follow the paths indicated in the diagram, keeping well on-side until they know that the kick has been made. Full-back goes straight to the opposing end.

This play can only be executed from the left side of the field, and the kick should be high enough to enable the right end to get under it and capture it if possible before it reaches the ground. Failing to do this, if close pressed by the opposing end, he should leave the ball to be secured by his own left guard or half-back, and himself vigorously engage the end.

An Illustration of the quarterback kick in Camp and Deland (1896).

The receiving teams soon realized that if they kept the kicker from running downfield, he could not place his teammates back onside, so the receiving team aligned players to knock down the kicker to prevent him from running downfield. This tactic became known as **roughing** the kicker.

The onside kick from placement or kickoff also originated in the 1890s. Before 1894, the kicking team was the team that had been scored on. As in soccer, the kicking team could dribble kick a few feet, pick up the ball, and run with it. That changed in 1894 when a new rule required kickoffs to travel at least ten yards before the kicking team could recover the ball. Under the new rule, kicking teams began booting the ball far downfield, so receiving teams moved their men back to block for the teammate that received the kick.

That was the case when Pop Warner, Georgia's coach, scouted the John Heisman-led Auburn team before their 1896 Thanksgiving Day rivalry game. Warner saw that Auburn had one player positioned about ten yards from the kicker and the others standing further back. So, Warner took advantage of Auburn's alignment by kicking the ball short and toward the sideline, where Georgia recovered after it traveled ten yards. And so, the onside kick from placement was born.

Hike and Hard Count

As in rugby, centers initially snapped the ball by rolling it under one foot. By 1892, centers used their hands to roll the ball to the quarterback, who squatted behind the center. Next, centers started tossing the ball to the quarterback; others handed it to him. Whatever the technique, offenses needed a mechanism to tell the center when to snap the ball. Initially, that involved the quarterback touching the center's thigh to request the ball.

A 1905 Minnesota yearbook illustration shows one of the
common positions taken by quarterbacks to receive the snap.
(1905 University of Minnesota *Gopher*)

Since football did not have a neutral zone until 1906, defenders sometimes reached across the line and touched the center's thigh, causing an
early snap. When that trick happened to John Heisman's Auburn team in
the late 1890s, he had his quarterback switch to the verbal command,
"Hike." Auburn's opponents caught on, coming off the ball as quickly as
Auburn, so Heisman sometimes had the ball snapped on the second
"Hike," drawing defenders offside. Today, quarterbacks draw defenders
offside by emphasizing certain parts of their cadence, a practice called a
hard count since the early 1980s.

Subsequently, teams created any number of coded signal systems to call
the play and the snap count, and hiking the ball became synonymous with
snapping the ball.

Field General

From its beginning, football captains led their teams before giving way to
volunteer and professional coaches. The captain-led model held on
among some Eastern teams into the 1910s while coaches took control
elsewhere. Still, despite coaches managing practices, outlining game
strategies, and handling game substitutions, the game's tradition and rule
prohibited coaching from the sideline. Coaches, players, and fans were
barred from shouting instructions or signaling plays to players on the
field.

The situation placed great responsibility on team captains and quarter-backs to manage the team. Like military leaders who were effective on the battlefield, heady or inspirational quarterbacks were called **field generals** starting in 1893.

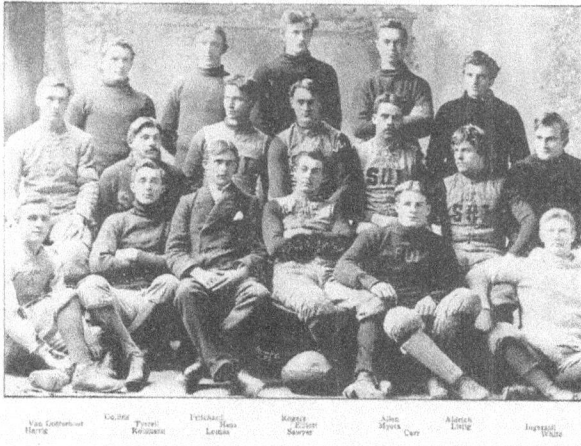

Quarterback Prince Sawyer, the first football player to be called a field general, sits in the middle of the front row with Iowa's 1893 team. (1895 University of Iowa *Hawkeye*)

Point of Attack, Shift, Shifted and Unbalanced Formations, Strong and Weak Side

As football play became increasingly structured, many of the game's early and influential strategists viewed football tactics through a military lens. Among them were Lt. C. A. L. Totten, an Army officer who taught Military Science and Tactics at Yale from 1889 to 1892, and Lorin F. Deland, a military historian by avocation who advised Harvard during the same period, co-authoring *Football* with Walter Camp in 1896.

When the *New York Mail and Express* asked Totten to analyze the 1891 Yale-Princeton game, he argued that offensive plays were akin to military movements in their use of surprise and movement to gain a numerical advantage.

> If we can conceal our real intention and deceive the enemy respecting the true **point of attack**, success will be more certain, and, at any rate, more decisive.

Initial formational alignments, shifts, and post-snap movements combined to bring more offensive players to the point of attack than the defense had.[2]

Offenses used their initial alignment, pre-snap movements, and post-snap movements to gain an advantage. For example, Carlisle aligned with more players on one side of the ball than the other in 1899. Likewise, Yost's 1905 *Football for Player and Spectator* included the Tackle Over formation with the nominal left tackle aligned outside the right tackle and vice versa. In other formations, Yost set more backs to one side of the ball than the other.

Since early football had few limits on the number of players on the line of scrimmage or in motion, teams put players in motion before the snap to overwhelm the defenders at the called hole. An 1894 rule capped the number of players in motion at three to limit these attacks, and a 1903 rule required offenses to have seven players on the line of scrimmage. These limitations on player movements led to the use of pre-snap **shifts**. Stagg often receives credit for developing the first shift; however, Pop Warner's Wing Shift, which Carlisle executed in their 45-0 win over Columbia in 1899, appears to have been the first.

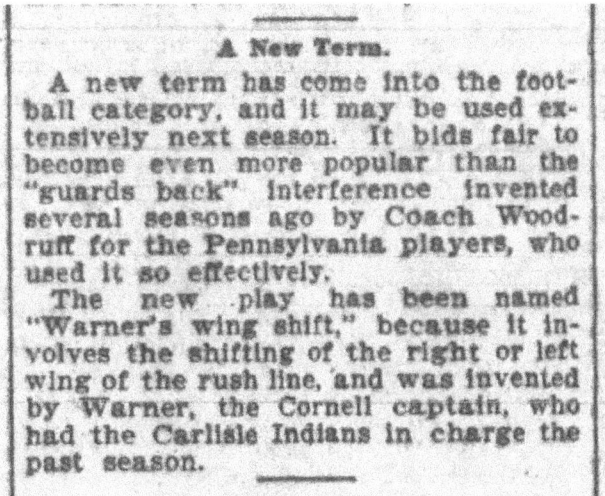

A New Term.

A new term has come into the football category, and it may be used extensively next season. It bids fair to become even more popular than the "guards back" interference invented several seasons ago by Coach Woodruff for the Pennsylvania players, who used it so effectively.

The new play has been named "Warner's wing shift," because it involves the shifting of the right or left wing of the rush line, and was invented by Warner, the Cornell captain, who had the Carlisle Indians in charge the past season.

Other articles of the ea noted Warner's innovation, while a Montana newspaper told readers Warner added a new term to football's lexicon. ('A New Term,' *Anaconda Standard*, December 24, 1899.)

Next came H. L. Williams' Minnesota Shift, in which all but the center initially aligned behind the line of scrimmage before shifting in unison, ending with more players on one side of the center than the other. They paused briefly before the snap so they were not in motion. Defenses had difficulty adjusting to a well-executed shift, so some had their linemen remain standing to more easily shift horizontally based on the offensive movements.

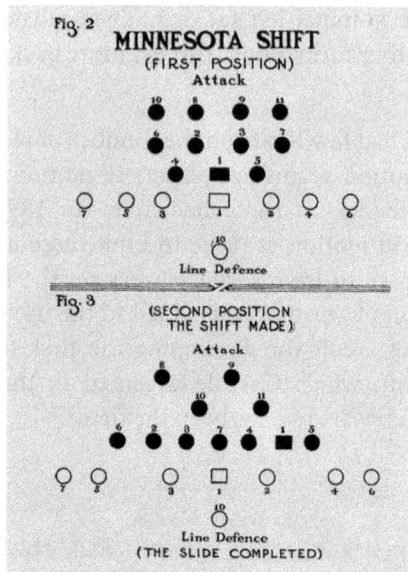

The Minnesota Shift had multiple variations that resulted in an unbalanced formation. (Reed, 1913)

Formations with uneven numbers of players on either side of the center became known as **shifted formations** or *lopsided formations*. However, after the Single Wing teams of the 1910s team began lining up in uneven numbers (without shifting), **unbalanced formation** became the accepted terminology.

On a related note, American football in the 1800s continued using the Britishism "side" to describe a team, so a strong football team was often called a strong side. However, around 1915, teams in unbalanced formations began referring to the side of the ball with more players than the other as the **strong side**, while the side with fewer players was the **weak side.**

. . .

Straight Arm and Stiff Arm

The first American football rules did not differentiate between the offense and defense using their hands and arms. However, both sides were restricted from holding, slugging (punching), or tripping opponents. Then, as a tradeoff for the offense being allowed to block and control the ball for multiple downs, an 1888 rule made the ball carrier the only offensive player who could use their hands and arms to ward off opponents. Other offensive players had to keep their hands to themselves.

The runner's ability to use his hands and arms was more significant back then because tackling had to be above the waist. An 1888 rule allowed tackling above the knees, so runners used an extended arm to keep potential tacklers away from their torsos and thighs. Called a **straight arm** by 1891 and a **stiff arm** by 1895, the terms became interchangeable.

Ransome Making His Long Run, With Cochrane Waiting to Tackle Him.

Cal's A. W. Ransome stiff arms Stanford's Guy Cochran in the 1895 Big Game. ('Was Six To Half Dozen,' *San Francisco Examiner*, November 29, 1895.)

Broken Field Runner and Broken Play

Charles Darwin popularized "broken field" in *The Voyage of the Beagle* when he described landing on Chatham Island in the Galapagos Archipelago and finding "a broken field of black basaltic lava, thrown into the most rugged waves, and crossed by great fissures."[3] Presumably, the rugged nature of the island's field was analogous to the obstacles faced by a ball carrier. Runners who avoid tacklers while speedily making their way downfield have been called **broken field runners** since the 1890s.

Perhaps originating from the same branch of the word tree, offensive plays that do not operate properly due to offensive mistakes became known as **broken plays** in the 1920s.

Criss-Cross, Trick Play, End Around, Crossbuck, Reverse, Misdirection, and Counter

Plays of the late 1880s appear strange to modern eyes. Teams had varying numbers of players on the line of scrimmage and multiple men in motion at the snap, some of whom were moving forward. However, the strangest element was that nearly every play had three or more blockers preceding the ball carrier through the hole. While the concentration of blockers made it difficult for the defenders at the point of attack, the plays were easy for defenders to read: wherever the blockers went, so went the ball.

That tendency led to change of direction plays, specifically the **criss-cross** that premiered in the 1888 Phillips Andover-Phillips Exeter game. The criss-cross had Andover's quarterback, Lou Owsley, toss the ball to Laurie Bliss, who started around the end before tossing the ball to his brother, Cliff Bliss, running in the opposite direction. The criss-cross innovation quickly spread across the country.

Camp and Deland (1896) were careful to distinguish the criss-cross and double pass, saying:

> By this term "double pass" we here mean either criss-cross or double pass, for it is general among players to distinguish these two by using the term "double pass" with the meaning that the ball be passed in the same general direction; while by "criss-cross" is meant a pass whereby the ball is then carried by the second runner in the opposite direction of the moving mass of men, ...[4]

Fake punts, fake field goals, and plays designed to deceive the defense by sending some players in one direction and the ball in the other became known as **trick plays** in the 1890s, while plays that did not use deceptions were *straight plays* or *straight football*. Still, without the threat of the forward pass, teams had limited means of deceiving defenders, so they continually sought better ways to overpower the defense at the point of attack.

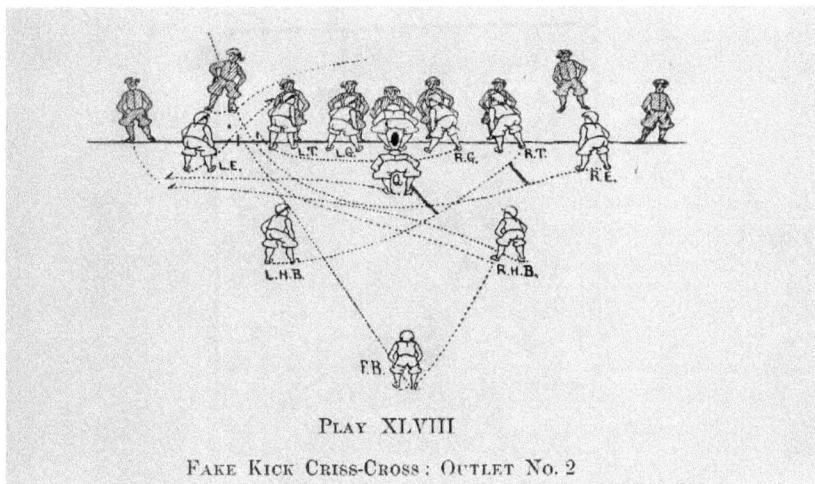

PLAY XLVIII

FAKE KICK CRISS-CROSS: OUTLET NO. 2

Walter Camp and Lorin Demand wrote about the strategy of trick plays in 1896.
This criss-cross play went to the left halfback, who handed it to the right end.
(Camp and Deland, 1896)

A more basic play was the buck or line buck, in which the quarterback received the snap and passed it to a back who ran straight into the designated point in the interior line, much like today's dive play. Of course, defenses reacted to the movement of the blockers by reinforcing the point of attack. That led 1890s offenses to fake the buck to a back running in one direction and give the ball to a teammate heading in the opposite direction. Unlike the criss-cross, which involved two passes, the **cross-buck** had only one.

Teams of the 1890s often gave the ball to guards, tackles, and ends on running plays around the opposite end. Those became known as guard arounds, tackle arounds, and **end arounds**, but rule changes have barred the first two, so only the end around survives today.

The use of the criss-cross term faded in the 1900s when the **reverse** arrived with Pop Warner's Single Wing. Warner unveiled the reverse in 1913 during Carlisle's 35-0 win over previously undefeated Dartmouth at the Polo Grounds. Warner's reverse from the Single Wing involved the tailback or fullback sweeping toward the Wing, who received the ball while heading in the opposite end, often with a guard or tackle as a lead blocker. Newspaper reports indicate Carlisle also executed double and triple passes during the game.

By SOL METZGER.

Sol Metzger argued the distinguishing feature of Warner's reverse was the blocker leading the back around the end. (Metzger, Sol, 'Quick Reverse Passes Make Play A Go,' *News and Observer* (*Charlotte, NC*), October 15, 1926.)

In addition to the plays already mentioned, the Notre Dame Box and other shifting formations of the 1910s and 1920s used intricate backfield movements such as side steps and spins, a combination of tactics Knute Rockne called **misdirection**:

> Any successful attack in this modern game must be based largely upon fine blocking and the element of misdirection. .. I have used the shift because it helped along the lines of misdirection -of threatening one spot and then striking at another.[5]

Finally, the arrival of the Modern T formation in 1940 led to misdirection plays that sent one halfback in motion across the formation while handing off to the other halfback running off tackle away from the motion man. While similar in concept to crossbucks, such plays were called **counters** in T formation terminology.

Defensive End

Until two-platoon football came along, players were known by their offensive position. An end was an end regardless of whether the team was on offense or defense. Still, some players were better on offense or defense, and the skills and responsibilities differed between the two, so there was some need to distinguish the play of ends on offense and defense. Interestingly, the first appearance of **defensive end** in print came in a description of the Orange Athletic Club in their 1890 game against Harvard:

> Orange was especially strong in her defensive end play. The fact they had Stagg and Bovaird, two first-class Yale and Princeton end rushers, kept Harvard from running up the score to more than half what it might otherwise have been.[6]

So, Amos Alonzo Stagg, who played for Orange AC after he graduated from Yale, was among the first football players described as playing defensive end.

Primary Defense, Secondary Defense, and Defensive Secondary

Even before the forward pass, commentators recognized that defenses, like offenses, had players positioned at multiple levels from the line of scrimmage. Most defenses of the time had seven players on the line of scrimmage with four backs aligned at varying distances from the ball. Since the linemen and backs represented different levels of defense, the linemen were referred to as the **primary defense** and the backs as the **secondary defense**. (Some coaches discussed secondary and tertiary defensive levels as well.)

7-3-1 Defense

QB

RHB   FB   LHB

RE   T   G   C   G   T   LE

○ ○ ○ ⊗ ○ ○ ○

○

○ ○ ○

Players' offensive positions commonly defined their defensive roles.

Primary defense soon fell out of use, but the secondary defense morphed by 1918 to become **defensive secondary** while continuing to refer to the backs on defense.

Nose Guard, Mouth Guard, Face Mask, and Facemasking

As football became increasingly rough and played in close quarters, more than a few players suffered broken noses and other facial injuries. Attempting to limit those injuries, Arthur Cumnock, Harvard's captain in 1892, developed a rubber device that strapped around the head while clenched between the teeth via a shelf on its backside. Cumnock's device was called a **nose guard** by almost everyone.

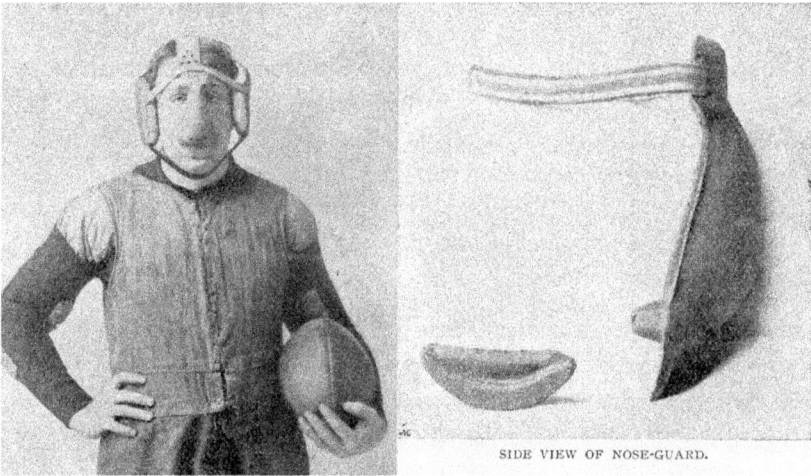

SIDE VIEW OF NOSE-GUARD.

A player wears an early head harness and nose guard. The profile view of the device shows the shelf or mouthpiece. (Cook, Charles Emerson. 'Football in Armour,' *Strand*, March 1897)

Cumnock sold his rights to the nose guard to John Morrill, who modified and commercialized it, so it became Morrill's Nose Guard. Those who did not want to wear the full nose guard could only use the **mouth guard**.

Competitors developed similar products and, perhaps to differentiate their product from Morrill's, or because some versions covered the cheeks, the Victor brand referred to their device as a **face mask** by 1897.

Nose guards remained the dominant term for all such devices until the 1920s. By then, the strap-on nose guards were out of style, and full-face executioner's masks took their turn protecting players' faces. The 1930s saw the first use of bird-cage-style devices resembling today's face masks. Due to concerns that face masks blocked the wearer's vision or injured other players, many alternative designs came on the market in the 1950s before football settled on the cage style used today.

The NCAA, junior colleges, and high schools made it illegal to grasp another player's face mask in 1957, and the NFL did so in 1962. Still, **face-masking** did not appear in print until 1962, and its non-hyphenated form took another five or six years to appear.

Shoulder Pads

As mass and momentum plays took over football in the 1890s, players protected their upper bodies with homemade pads stuffed with cotton, wool, or hair sewn inside or outside their jerseys. The number of pads and location depended on each player's position, injury history, and preferences. Some padded their sternum, elbows, or forearms, with padded shoulders being the most common. Commercially produced, stuffed leather pads soon followed.

An 1894 newspaper article, 'Armor for Football,' which covered all elements of protective gear worn by football players, did not mention shoulder pads. The first mention of **shoulder pads** came in an 1895 report on the Yale-Orange Athletic Club (of Newark) game played one week before the Yale-Princeton contest. The *New York Sun* reporter described the unusual gear worn by some Yale players:

> The Yale men wore more headgear and harness than has ever been seen in this city. The backs wore leather helmets with ear protectors and rubber nose masks, so their friends were utterly unable to recognize them from the grand stand. The men in the line, especially Chadwick and Murphy, wore immense pads on their shoulders and arms, while none failed to have on shin guards. Chadwick wore what looked like a saddle on his left shoulder, and his head was bound in rubber bandages. He was not suffering from any recent injuries, but was simply unwilling to take chances. With the Princeton game only a week off, the New Haven boys knew that an injury to one of their men might turn the tide of victory or defeat, and recognizing the roughness that might be encountered in a battle with Orange, they came well fortified against accidents.[7]

The image of the 1895 Yale football team includes three players with shoulder pads, including #7 captain S.B. Thorne holding the ball, #8 C. Chadwick, over Thorne's left shoulder, and #10 Bass, second from the right. (Pach Brothers, Outing, Wiki)

By the end of the 1895 season, other Yale players wore shoulder pads, as did at least one Princeton player. Shoulder pads crossed the continent by the 1896 season when Randall Ludlow of Cal wore them.

Headgear, Head Harness, Chin Strap, and Helmet

Just as players began padding their bodies and legs as football got rougher, they also covered their heads. Gone were skull and stocking caps. Instead, players grew their hair long, with some wrapping their heads with bandages to protect their ears.

In 1894, they began wearing custom **head harnesses** or **headgear** with felt muffs for ear protection, similar to today's wrestling headgear. First made on a custom basis by the local harness maker, the sporting goods folks followed suit, and the head protectors became popular among players who needed them. But, unfortunately, most didn't think they did.

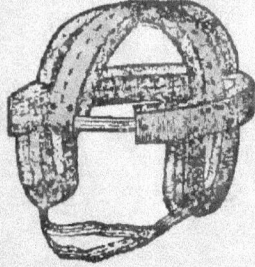

Spalding's Head Harness

(PATENTED.

This style head harness is the lightest and most comfortable to wear of any head guard yet devised. It is made of tan leather and thoroughly padded with wool felt a half-inch thick, with an elastic to go under the chin, and is adjustable to any size head. It is a thorough protection to the crown and back of the head, also to the ears.

No. 35. Each, $2.25

The Spalding's Head Harness had been through several seasons when this version was on the market. (1899 Official Foot Ball Guide)

The following year players at Yale wore **helmets**, distinguished from harnesses and headgear by a cap or shell offering mechanical protection. However, using sole leather violated football's rule banning equipment made of hard substances, so helmets were soon banned. Nevertheless, "helmet" became a common, though inaccurate, term for leather and fabric head harnesses.

ELY, YALE'S QUARTER-BACK, COMPLETELY EQUIPPED WITH PROTECTIVE APPLIANCES

Yale's quarterback, Ely, wears a nose guard and helmet. (*Collier's Weekly*, September 23, 1899)

Meanwhile, a 1904 head harness advertisement mentioned that their product had "elastic to go under the chin," which they called a **chin strap**.

Scrub and First String

Football practices have long benefitted from teams having enough players to allow full scrimmages. Since early varsity teams often had small rosters, schools had student volunteers or **scrubs** compete with the varsity in practice. (Previously, scrubs are less desirable livestock, while open track meets sometimes included contests for untrained participants, called scrub races.)

The earliest use of "scrub" tied to football came following two weeks of preseason workouts for the 1884 Princeton team. The team captain selected eleven varsity members, with others forming a scrub team. For the next 75 years, many college yearbooks saluted the scrubs by devoting a page to extoll their efforts.

THE SCRUBS

There was once a team called the Scrubs,
Mostly picked from a bunch of dubs,
But under Coach Bill
They worked with a will,
And next year they will make good subs.

Tulane's 1919 scrub team earned a picture, poem, and other text honoring their achievements. (1920 Tulane *Jambalaya*)

Teams with more than eleven players on their rosters had to distinguish between the eleven who started the game and those who did not. Around

1900, football borrowed **first string** from track and field, a term that designated a school's best athlete for meets that allowed schools one entry per event. In turn, track and field had borrowed the term from medieval archers who carried a replacement string in case their first string broke.

Safety and Linebacker

Players held the same offensive and defensive positions until two-platoon football came along. Most defensive position names did not arrive until the 1950s, though some terminology was developed to describe defensive alignment and techniques. For example, during football's first few decades, players on the defensive line were called rushers or the rush line, and the defenders positioned slightly behind the rush line were *rush line backs*. The deep man on defense, often the quarterback or fullback, returned punts and was the last man available to tackle a breakaway runner, leading them to be described as playing **safety**.

Likewise, some teams shifted their center on defense from the defensive line to a spot standing a yard to two off the line of scrimmage. The approach came to be known as the *roving center*, *backer-up*, or **line-backer** by 1895. Of course, some centers were ill-suited to the roving center or line-backing role, so they switched spots with a guard, tackle, or fullback while on defense, divorcing a player's offensive position from their defensive position.

Training Camp

Football seasons of the past began as they do today with several weeks of preseason practice, but there were differences as well. First, before the 1960s, college football teams seldom started their seasons before October, so preseason training began in early September. Second, year-round conditioning was not standard, so athletic teams (e.g., major league baseball) and individuals (e.g., boxers and cyclists) often spent the first portion of their preseason practice on conditioning. Third, these conditioning practices often occurred in rustic locations lacking potential distractions or permanent facilities, so teams pitched tents at their **training camps**.

Beginning in the mid-1910s, Pop Warner's Pitt team created a tent city at Camp
Hamilton near Winter, PA. (Personal collection)

Remote training camps for football started in the 1890s, with Nebraska
being an early adopter. Soon, nearly every program encamped before the
season. The camps began with extended walks, runs, calisthenics, and
non-contact drills such as falling on the football, all capped off by ample
time spent at the swimming hole.

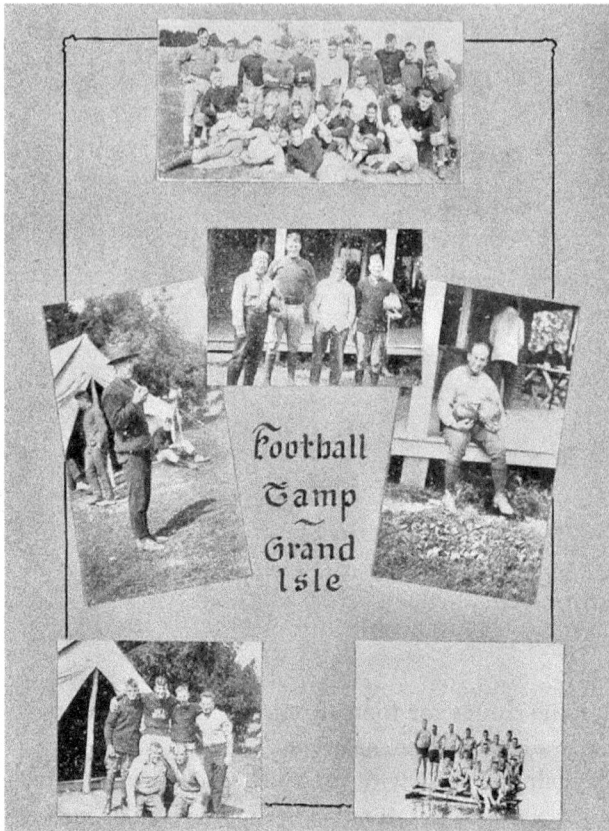

Vermont's 1920 training camp included various conditioning and football activities and plenty of time cooling off in the water.
(1921 University of Vermont *Ariel*)

Perhaps the most notable accomplishment by a team in training camp came in 1906 when St. Louis University camped near Lake Beulah, Wisconsin. St. Louis U's head coach, Eddie Cochems, used the training camp to test his ideas for the newly-legalized forward pass. Before returning to St. Louis, Cochems took his team one county north to play Carroll University, where St. Louis' Bradbury Robinson threw the first legal forward pass in a regular-season game. Unfortunately, it went incomplete, though St. Louis completed several others that day, including one touchdown pass.

· · ·

Tackling Dummy

When football's rules changed in 1888 to allow tackling above the knees, the rules explicitly defined "unnecessary roughness" as hacking, throttling, butting, tripping up, intentional tackling below the knees, and striking with a closed fist. Princeton's captain, Hector Cowan, magnified the importance of tackling above the knee by being disqualified for illegal tackling during the 1888 Yale-Princeton game.

Teaching proper tackling was sufficiently important that the captains of the 1899 Yale and Harvard teams independently developed tools to teach good tackling form. For example, Amos Alonzo Stagg, Yale's captain, rolled up a mattress, suspended it from the gym's ceiling, and scattered other mattresses on the floor so players could practice tackling without fear of injury.

The same season and 135 miles northeast, Harvard's captain, Arthur Cumnock, created a similar apparatus. Cumnock hung a heavy log 10 inches in diameter and 5 feet 9 inches tall with a metal band corresponding to a ball carrier's waist. As a newspaper reporter explained at the time:

> The thing is hung from the ceiling by a (sic) pully rope, which is manipulated by one of the substitutes. When the imaginary rusher is swinging freely in the air the Harvard rusher running at full speed, seizes it at the cross-piece, throws his weight against it, gives it a sharp twist or two with his arms and downs it to the soft turf.[8]

The article's subtitle was *Harvard's Foot-Ball Players Practice With a Dummy Rusher*. Whether the Harvard players referred to the log as a dummy or the sportswriter coined the term, inanimate bags of rags, sawdust, and other materials have been **tackling dummies** ever since.

Chains and Chain Gang

Football introduced the system of downs in 1882, which required teams to advance the ball five yards in three downs. How the game's officials kept track of where each set of downs began or the spot needed to gain is unclear, though some reports indicate that umpires placed a handkerchief at the spot to gain.

It took a dozen years, but someone associated with the Crescent Athletic Club of Brooklyn had the idea to track the yards to gain using a tool positioned along the sideline. Crescent connected two rods with a string or rope five yards long and set one end at the first down spot and the other at the yard to gain.

A few weeks later, the new tool gained mention leading up to the Harvard-Yale game in Springfield. The teams agreed to have George Pratt, a former Amherst player and captain of the Crescent Athletic Club, serve as the game's linesman. They also named an assistant linesman:

> ...in order that there may be no question in regard to the distance gained and lost by teams, a piece of tape five yards long will be stretched between two rods and each of the linesmen will look after one end.[9]

Word of the invention reached the Midwest by March 1895, since the schools that became the Big Ten amended the Eastern football rules so that: "... a substitute for each team act as a linesman and they shall use a line five yards long with a stake at each end."[10]

However, it was not until 1898 that the East updated their rules to require two linesman's assistants to manage the "two light poles about six feet in length and connected at the lower ends by a stout cord or chain exactly five yards long.

The shows two assistant linesmen. One is a civilian, and the other is a Naval Academy substitute player. (1911 United States Naval Academy *Lucky Bag*)

The individuals working the chains were known simply as the assistant linesmen until the early 1920s, when it became acceptable in polite company, or, at least, in the newspapers, to refer to them as the **chain gang.**

Conference

Among the core themes in football history has been the shifting power vested in individual teams, leagues, and governing bodies. When the IFA, Eastern football's rule-making body, splintered in the 1890s, Western schools opted to make their own rules.

Michigan, Minnesota, Northwestern, and Wisconsin formed the Intercollegiate Association of the Northwest (IAAN) in 1892 to coordinate football, baseball, and track competitions among the schools, but it folded after only two years. Likewise, Sewanee (University of the South), Alabama, Auburn, Georgia, and Vanderbilt formed the Southern Intercollegiate Athletic Association (SIAA) in 1895.

The faculties of the Midwestern schools that had formed the IAAN in 1982 agreed in 1895 to hold a meeting or **conference** with the faculties of similar schools to establish athletic policies. Officially known as the Intercollegiate Conference of Faculty Representatives (aka the Western Conference), it continues today as the Big Ten. From a terminology standpoint, however, their meetings provided the basis for collections of schools with organized athletic relationships to be called conferences.

Mascot

Military units and other organizations have long had pets to entertain and comfort unit members, but it was not until the 1880s that **mascot** entered the English language. The term came from a popular opera, *La Mascotte*, that concerned a farm girl whose presence brought bountiful crops to her farmer employer so long as the girl remained a virgin. It is unclear how long the farmer enjoyed bountiful harvests, but "mascot" quickly described a person or animal that brings good fortune.

Campus dogs were common mascots for college football teams. Yale's Handsome Dan, a bulldog that appeared at games as early as 1890, was the first college mascot. Later Yale mascots included dogs of other breeds, but the Elis ultimately chose Bulldogs as their team nickname, and all subsequent mascots have been bulldogs named Handsome Dan.

Army's costumed mule appeared at the Polo Grounds during their 1913 win over Navy. (George Grantham Bain Collection, Library of Congress)

Navy has used a goat as its mascot since 1893. Unfortunately, the night before the 1912 Army-Navy game, their goat died. Since Navy won the game the following day, a debate arose before the 1913 game on the advisability of sacrificing their new goat to ensure victory. Alas, the goat survived the day, and Navy lost the game, but the loss might have resulted from a college football first, the appearance of a costumed mascot on the Army sideline.

Home and Away Games

Due to travel challenges, it was not unusual for early football teams to play one another at neutral locations partway between the two schools. However, most games involved teams located near one another, with the teams alternating the game location from year to year.

Reporting on baseball teams and their schedules referred to teams playing **home games** in the 1880s, and that term carried over to football by 1890. However, football did not have a consistent term describing games played at the other team's campus.

The Schedule

AT HOME

September 24	Syracuse	0	St. Bonaventure	0
October 8	Syracuse	6	Rochester	0
October 15	Syracuse	14	Carlisle Indians	0
October 22	Syracuse	12	Hobart	5
October 29	Syracuse	0	Michigan	11
November 5	Syracuse	3	Vermont	0
November 12	Syracuse	6	Colgate	11

ABROAD

October 1	Syracuse	6	Yale	12
November 19	Syracuse	0	Illinois	3
November 24	Syracuse	6	St. Louis	0

One Hundred Eighty-seven

According to their yearbook staff, Syracuse played seven games at home and three abroad in 1910. (1912 Syracuse University *Onondagan*)

The term "away game" appeared in the 1910s, primarily concerning English and some American soccer matches. The expression transferred to basketball in the 1920s, before **away game** reached football in the 1930s.

All America

During the 1870s and 1880s, traveling show promoters claimed that each member of their troupe was a star; they were "all stars." That terminology leaked into the sporting world when Albert Spalding promoted a world tour following baseball's 1888 season. The tour included demonstration games between Spalding's Chicago White Stockings and the All Americans, a team comprised of players from various professional teams. Starting in Chicago, the tour traveled west, continuing to Hawaii, Australia, Egypt, and Europe before returning to New York and other parts of the Eastern U.S.

The world tour took the Chicago White Stockings and the All Americans to the Sphinx. (P. Sebah, National Baseball Hall of Fame)

Borrowing the name, Casper Whitney, a top sportswriter of the era and publisher of *This Week's Sports*, published an All-America football team after the 1889 season. All eleven players named to the team played for Yale, Princeton, or Harvard, establishing the trend of Eastern players dominating All-America teams until WWI.

CLASSIFYING FOOTBALL PLAYERS is not so simple as it looks. It should be borne in mind that the opinions advanced in this column are the results of a season's work. The men are not chosen for the national team from their showing in any one game, but from what they have done throughout the football year. Bearing this in mind, therefore, I should pick the All America eleven of '91 as follows:

Homans, full back.
McClung and Lake, half backs.
King, quarter.
Adams, centre.
Heffelfinger and Riggs, guards.
Newell and Winter, tackles.
Hinkey and Hartwell, ends.

SUBSTITUTES.

Poe, Bliss, Barbour, and Trafford behind the line.
Holly, Balliet, Warren, Hallowell, and Newton in the line.

It may be interesting, and serve for matter of record as well, to reproduce here the All America teams of '90 and '89.

That of '90 was:

Homans, full back.
McClung and Corbett, half backs.
Dean, quarter.
Cranston, centre.
Heffelfinger and Riggs, guards.
Rhodes and Newell, tackles.
Hallowell and Warren, ends.

SUBSTITUTES.

Hartwell, Upton, and Morison in the line.
Poe for quarter.
King, Lee, Lake, and Bliss for halves.
Trafford, full back.

That of '89 was:

Ames, full back.
Lee and Channing, half backs.
Poe, quarter.
George, centre.
Heffelfinger and Cranston, guards.
Cowan and Gill, tackles.
Cumnock and Stagg, ends.

SUBSTITUTES.

Dean, Trafford, Black, and McBride behind the line.
Janeway, Stickney, Donnelly, and Rhodes in the line.

The opening paragraphs of Whitney's 1891 article. He then describes the merits of each selected player. (Whitney, Caspar. 'Amateur Sport,' *Harper's Weekly*, December 12, 1891.)

Whitney's publication soon failed, so he and the All-America team transferred to *Harper's Weekly* in 1890. Walter Camp took over naming the team from 1897 to 1924. Following Camp's death in 1925, Grantland Rice named the teams until 1953.

3

THE NINETEEN AUGHTS

Charging Machine, Blocking Machine, and Blocking Sled

Coaches have consistently sought ways for players to practice football without hitting one another. One of the iconic tools for doing so was the **charging machine**, first mentioned in reports about Cornell's practices in 1900. Their coach, Percy Haughton, apparently borrowed the idea for the charging machine from his alma mater, Harvard, though it is unclear when Harvard first used one. Early charging machines, used for defensive drills, rested on wheels or skids and had a long, horizontal plank covered with padded leather. Linemen drove their hands into the padded plank, pushing the contraption until the coach thought their performance satisfactory. It seldom was.

A group of linemen spent an enjoyable afternoon pushing a heavy wooden object around an open field. (Edwards, 1916)

A variation of the charging machine soon came into use to practice blocking. Rather than having a long horizontal board, the **blocking machine** had five or seven vertical pads, allowing multiple linemen to practice their drive blocking. Princeton's 1902 version even had leather heads protruding from the pads to simulate the opposition better.

Early machines were homemade and built of wood, but commercially produced metal sleds became available in the 1930s when the devices became known as **blocking sleds**.

Chalk Talk

Before dry-erase boards and PowerPoint, people with something to say often illustrated their presentations using blackboards and chalk. Presentations given on topics ranging from religion, temperance, science, and art were called **chalk talks** in the 1880s and 1890s.

The first known connection to football came in 1898 when an old football player gave a chalk talk to the Pittsfield (MA) High School team before their season. We do not know the contents of that chalk talk, but given the time and situation, it may have been about football's rules and strategies rather than details about plays. Nebraska's coach, Walter Booth, gave chalk talks to students and others in 1900 and 1901. However, the first chalk talks known to be delivered by a coach to his team were by Minnesota's H. L. Williams in 1904.

One of the worst chalk talks ever came in 1904 when Wes Clapp delivered a chalk talk to his Kalamazoo College team a week before their game with Michigan. Michigan had shut out Case (33-0) and Ohio Northern (48-0) in the first two weeks of the season, and Kalamazoo was up next. But, unlike many coaches who would provide their team with some reason or sliver of hope for victory, Clapp went the opposite direction, saying:

> I want you to watch every play your opponent makes and see if you can not profit by it. Don't go into the game with the idea that you can score on them, for teams a great deal better than Kalamazoo have failed to do that. Go into the game, however, to keep the score against us as low as possible.[1]

Clapp proved correct in predicting that Kalamazoo would not score on Michigan, but was overly optimistic about the Hornets keeping the score low. Instead, they lost 95-0, a disappointment despite it being better than the 130-0 licking West Virginia absorbed two weeks later.

Off Tackle

It seems fitting that the first three instances of runs made "off tackle" involved Big Ten teams. Spaced a few weeks apart in November 1900, the first came in the Iowa-Chicago game when:

> Iowa began its attack on the ends and *just off the tackle*, and steadily pushed the ball down the field.[2]

Then, about two weeks later, as Northwestern prepared for the contest with Minnesota, a report mentioned that:

> Hollister's men practiced a new mass play *off the tackle* which may prove to be a puzzle to the husky linemen of the gopher eleven next Saturday.[3]

The final step came at the end of the month in a report on the Northwestern-Iowa game, indicating Northwestern's right halfback:

Godioz [G. O. Dietz] was sent twice in succession **off tackle** for another
first down, but wilted when called on another time.[4]

Although the Northwestern-Iowa game ended in a 5 to 5 tie, Big Ten and
other running backs have run plays off tackle ever since.

Checkerboard Field

Like rugby, early football did not allow the player receiving the snap to
run with the ball until another player had possessed it. But a 1903 rule
change gave offenses more flexibility by allowing that player to run with
the ball, provided he crossed the line of scrimmage five yards to the right
or left of the center. Some opposed the rule, so a compromise solution
applied the rule only between the 25-yard lines. As an aid for game officials to assess compliance, stripes were added to the field, running
perpendicular to the yard lines and five yards apart.

Field Dimensions and Markings (1903)

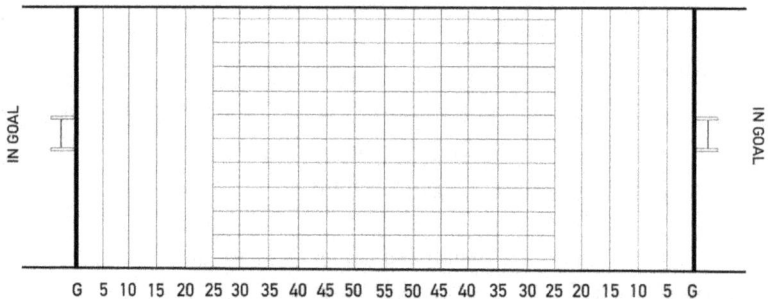

G 5 10 15 20 25 30 35 40 45 50 55 50 45 40 35 30 25 20 15 10 5 G

Football field markings in 1903 were a partial checkerboard.

The rule changed in 1904 to apply to the entire field, so the perpendicular
lines extended the field's length, making the field resemble a **checkerboard**. When the rule changed again in 1910 to remove the restrictions
on the player receiving the snap, the field markings returned to their
gridiron glory.

Field Dimensions and Markings (1904-1909)

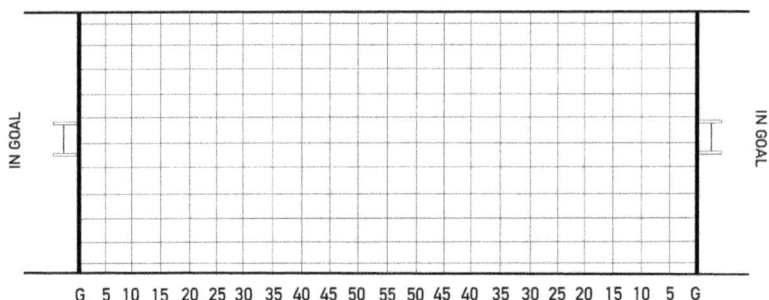

Football fields had a full checkerboard design from 1904 to 1909.

Kicking Shoe

Until the 1970s, the standard method of kicking a gridiron football was the straight-ahead, strike-with-the-toe approach. Early on, kickers wore standard shoes with cleats and rounded toes optimized for running and cutting. However, the cleats in the shoe's toe sometimes dug into the turf during a kicker's striking motion. In addition, the rounded toe made it more challenging to strike the ball true and send it straight ahead.

Newspaper reports mention that Penn's John Minds had a special kicking shoe in 1897, but its nature is unknown. The first player verified to have used a square-toed **kicking shoe** was Walter Eckersall, the University of Chicago's star halfback from 1903 to 1905. Eckersall's kicking shoe had a square toe and did not have cleats in the toe, ensuring a smooth path to the ball when kicking straight ahead.

Still, it took Harvard's Charles Brickley to popularize the square-toed attachment that slipped over the toe of his shoe when he booted five field goals in a 15-5 victory over Yale in 1913.

A period catalog featured the Brickley Kicking Toe that slipped over the toe of a football shoe. (c. 1915 James W. Brine Catalogue)

Line of Scrimmage and Neutral Zone

Just as players on opposing teams in a rugby scrum engage with one another, the same occurred in early football. The players on the line were supposed to remain behind the middle of the ball, but compliance was difficult to assess and enforce.

Differences in opinions about reducing mass and momentum play contributed to multiple rule-making bodies emerging in 1895, one of which required seven players to align on the **line of scrimmage**. This and similar rules helped reduce the game's violence over the next decade but still proved insufficient.

OLD STYLE "LINE UP"

NEW STYLE "LINE-UP"

The images illustrate how opposing lines faced one another before and after the introduction of the neutral zone. (1908 Dartmouth College *Aegis*)

The rules introduced in 1906 created a **neutral zone** between the two lines that only the offensive center could enter pre-snap. This rule gave the head linesman a clear line of sight to assess offside and other pre-snap fouls. It also meant football had two lines of scrimmage: a defensive line of scrimmage at the front and an offensive line of scrimmage at the back of the ball, which remains true today. Our Canadian friends really like their neutral zone. They require the defense to line up at least one yard from the ball.

Booster

Perhaps no word in football's vocabulary has more appropriate origins than **booster**. Originally, a booster was a shill or an accomplice in underhanded methods of separating marks from their money. They might, for example, work in a gambling house, winning often enough for marks to believe they were playing a fair game.

In the 1890s, boosting took on positive connotations when there was a fad to form boosters clubs that combined civic promotion and positive psychology. Boosting entered the football world in 1898 when an individual named O. B. Gillmore took the time to pen a three-stanza song extolling the virtues of the Ottawa football booster.

The dark side of football boosting arose in 1904 when a promising Nebraska football player revealed that a University of Chicago booster offered him money to transfer and play in the Windy City. Further, the article indicated that another Cornhusker received a similar offer in 1903. Since then, some boosters have been football's dark underbelly while others operate in the open to support their team through fundraising and other activities.

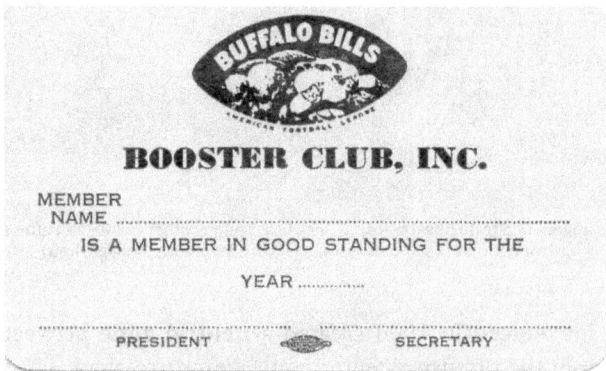

Some teams need more boosting than others. (Personal collection)

False Start

Football did not borrow many terms from horse racing and track and field, but the false start was one of them. In both forms of racing, a false start occurs when a competitor moves forward before the official gives the signal. At the turn of the last century, false starts in track led to disqualification on the third false start. The first two resulted in distance penalties in which the runner was set back from the starting line by a distance corresponding to the length of the race. The distance was one yard for races up to 125 yards, with the penalties ratcheting up until races over one mile had a ten-yard penalty. Racers earning a second false start doubled the distance from the line.

"False start" appears in some media reports in the 1890s to describe players being penalized for jumping offside on a scrimmage play. In 1903, however, there was a rash of offenses whose centers or other linemen deliberately moved before the snap to draw defensive players offside. At the time, an offensive lineman could shift or swap positions after placing their hand on the ground.

A rule, which passed in 1904 and came with a five-yard penalty, stated:

> If any player on the side in possession of the ball makes a deliberate attempt by a **false start** or otherwise to draw the opponents offside, the ball if then snapped shall not be regarded as in play or the scrimmage as begun.[5]

However, the rule changed in 1905 to distinguish the center from other linemen. Specifically, any ball movement by the center constituted a snap, putting the ball in play, while false starts remained dead ball penalties.

Pass and Forward Pass

Passing was common in football before the forward pass became legal in 1906. As a descendant of rugby, all methods of handing or tossing the ball to teammates were considered **passes**. For example, the football rules of 1876 included Rule 26:

> Throwing back. It is lawful for any player who has the ball to throw it backward toward his own goal, or to pass it back to any player of his side who is at the time behind him, in accordance with the rules of on side.[6]

Tossing the ball to a teammate behind the passer (positioned closer to their goal than the passer) ensured the ball went to an onside player. Of course, some passes went forward, but those were illegal, leading to the loss of possession when called.

Seeking to open up the game and give offenses more options to move the ball, the rule-makers of 1906 allowed tossing the ball to a teammate positioned forward of the passer (closer to the opponent's goal than the passer). Though heavily restricted, the **forward pass** was revolutionary because it violated the onside rule, a fundamental provision of previous kicking games.

. . .

Receive, Pass Receiving, Pass Reception, Receiving Yardage

Just as there were passes before the legal forward pass, those who caught the backward passes were sometimes said to **receive** the pass. So, it is no surprise that those catching forward passes were commended for their **pass-receiving** skills as early as 1907, though the first **pass reception** did not arrive until 1922. Likewise, it was not until 1942 that **receiving yardage** showed up, though its late arrival makes sense since the colleges did not keep official statistics until 1937.

Completed, Uncompleted, Incomplete Pass, and Incompletion

Following the legalization of the forward pass in 1906, reporters, and presumably coaches and players, did not have terms for passes that were caught or not. Caught passes were said to have worked, netted yards, or gained yardage. Passes that did not end up in the receiver's hands were said to have hit or fallen to the ground or failed to make the gain. Clearly, football needed some new words.

The 1907 rules committee came to the rescue by describing caught passes as being **completed**; those that were not were **uncompleted**.

SECTION 5. (a) After the ball has been legally passed forward, it may first be touched only by the player who received the ball from the snapper-back or such other players of the passer's side as were at the time that the ball was put in play at least 1 yard behind the line of scrimmage or were playing at either end of the said line.

Players who may receive forward pass.

If the forward pass is first touched by any other player of the passer's side the pass shall not be considered as completed.

PENALTY   (FIELD JUDGE)

For uncompleted pass the same as under Section 3 (a).

The passage from the 1907 rule book includes both complete and uncompleted passes. (1907 Spalding's Official Foot Ball Guide)

Although the rule book mentioned uncompleted passes, only a few reporters used the term in 1907; a few called them **incomplete** passes. However, most stuck to the lengthier descriptions of 1906 and continued using those expressions for another decade before complete and incomplete passes became the typical descriptors of the outcome of a forward pass.

A variation of the incomplete pass, the **incompletion**, appears once or twice before entering common use in the 1930s.

Interception, Picked Off, Pick, and Pick Six

Despite pre-1906 football allowing only backward passes, some backward passes were caught not by the intended receiver but by a defensive player. Needing a word to describe those instances, football settled on the term that described stopping a message from reaching its intended recipient: an **interception**. The term immediately transferred to defensive players catching forward passes in 1906.

Football borrowed another broadly used term that described the precise removal of bugs from plants, the shooting of birds, or the elimination of blockers and defenders on a football field. The term, of course, was **picked off**, which was first used to describe an interception in 1909. Nevertheless, it was not until the early 1980s that picked off transitioned to the noun form as players described getting a **pick**, and the century turned before the ultimate pick emerged: the **pick-six**. Used spottily in 2002, a 2002 analysis showed that NFL teams earning a pick-six won seventy-seven percent of their games, and the term soon became commonplace.

Screen Pass or Sucker Pass

Besides determining how to best throw and catch a football in 1906, coaches also had to figure out what to do with their offensive linemen, who were not eligible to catch a forward pass. What should they do, where should they go, and which blocking techniques should they use?

The new coach at Muskegon High School in Michigan, Bob Zuppke, came up with one approach. Like virtually every coach, he had difficulty identifying how his offensive line could protect that passer using only shoulder or screen blocks.

No. 24.
LEGAL USE OF ARMS BY PLAYER OF SIDE IN POSSESSION OF
THE BALL.
Player No. 2, in attempting to obstruct an opponent, is keeping his arms close
to his body. (See Rule 12—Explanation.)

An illustration from the 1906 rule book shows linemen could not use
their hands or extend their arms when blocking. (1906 Spalding's
Foot Ball Guide)

The 1906 rules did not restrict ineligible receivers from running downfield, so Zuppke sent his seven linemen downfield and protected the
passer with three backs. After taking a step or two downfield, one of the
offensive ends slipped behind the wall of offensive linemen and looked
for the pass from the quarterback. Although we do not know Zuppke's
name for the play, it became known as the **screen pass**, a term popularized by Ohio State's 1921 Rose Bowl team. The screen pass also became
known as the **sucker pass**, though that term largely disappeared by the
1990s.

Harvard's receiver catches a screen pass against Centre (wearing striped jerseys) in 1920. The chains on the far sideline indicate the offensive linemen were past the line of scrimmage as the receiver caught the pass. (Haughton, 1922)

A 1939 rule change allowed ineligible receivers to be downfield only on passes caught behind the line of scrimmage.

Tackle Eligible Pass

The rules legalizing the forward pass defined eligible receivers as the offensive backfield and the outermost player on the right and left sides of the line of scrimmage, typically the ends. Of course, other positions on the line could become eligible, given specific alignments and shifts.

Some teams experimented with formations placing the center over the ball, the quarterback five or more yards deep, and the other nine players spread across the field, just behind the line of scrimmage. Shortly before the snap, six players stepped onto the line of scrimmage, giving the defense little time to determine the eligible players.

Many saw these unconventional formations and movements as trickery rather than fundamental football, so new rules in 1915 required at least three backfield players to be five or more yards behind the line of scrimmage at the snap, effectively eliminating late shifts and these spread formations. Still, teams continued running trick plays, and the first such play described as a **tackle-eligible** was thrown by Notre Dame's George Gipp versus Michigan State in 1919.

Tackle-eligible plays reemerged when offenses began splitting one or both ends since defenses had difficulty judging whether the split end or tackle was the outermost player on the line of scrimmage. Once again, the football gods of the early 1950s considered this trickery, so the NFL declared players wearing numbers 50 through 79 to be ineligible. The NCAA did the same in 1955, reversing their decision in 1956 due to pressure from coaches like Bear Bryant, but even the Bear could not hold back the tide, and the NCAA reinstated the ban in 1967. Today, college players wearing ineligible receiver numbers are limited to catching the occasional backward pass. While backward passes look and feel like forward passes, they count as rushing yards in the game statistics.

Mousetrap Block or Trap Block

An enduring type of block takes advantage of a defensive player's aggressiveness by leaving him initially unblocked. After charging across the line, the defensive player gets sideswiped by a pulling blocker. Originally known as a "rat trap play" or **mousetrap block**, the maneuver was shortened to **trap block**.

Some argue that Pop Warner developed trap blocking or that it originated with Yale's "tackles back" formation. However, the evidence points to Harvard player and coach Percy Haughton, who learned a version of the mousetrap as a player under Guy Ayrault at Groton School in the early 1890s. Haughton popularized trap blocking during his time as Harvard's coach from 1908 to 1916.

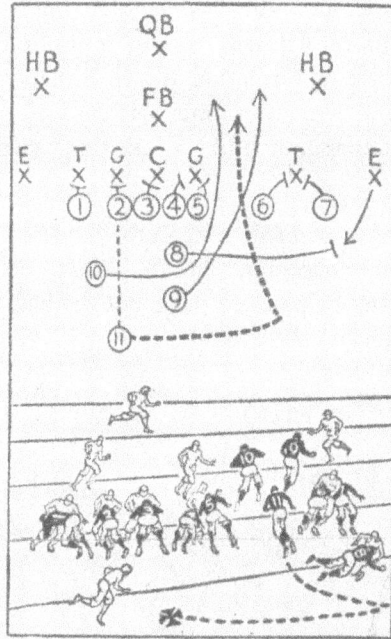

Yale's trap block had the quarterback trap or kick out the defensive
end. ('Yale Mouse-Trap Play Gains,' *Salt Lake City Tribune*, December
31, 1930.)

Quarterback Sneak

The **quarterback sneak** is among football's iconic plays. Every fan worth
their snow salt is familiar with Bart Starr sneaking behind Jerry Kramer
in the waning moments of the Ice Bowl to send the Packers to the first
Super Bowl. Yet, as Starr executed the play, the QB sneak is among the
game's simplest plays. The quarterback places his hands under center,
takes the snap, and drives on one side of the center, looking to gain a yard
or two. No handoffs. No fakes. Just a simple power play, so why is it
called a sneak?

The name results from the original quarterback sneak being a deception
play, not a power play. While there are references to quarterback sneaks
as early as 1903, the first documentation of the play's operation came
when Bo McMillan at Centre College and Pete Stinchcomb of Ohio State

ran it in 1917. Period descriptions of Stinchcomb's runs help explain the sneakiness of QB sneaks.

At the time, fullbacks or halfbacks handled the punting, with teams frequently punting on early downs from their punt formation, which they often used as their passing formation as well. Stinchcomb was an up back in Ohio State's punt formation, and his "sneaks" followed the center tossing him a short snap, much like a fake punt snapped to an up back today.

A play diagram shows a team aligning in the Double Wing with the quarterback offset from the center. Shortly before the snap, the fullback backpedals, suggesting he plans to punt, but the ball gets snapped to the quarterback, who runs it up the middle.

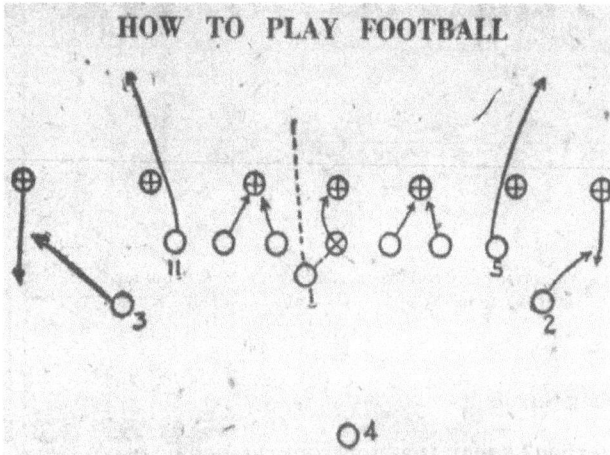

HOW TO PLAY FOOTBALL

An example of the original quarterback sneak. (Eckersall, Walter, 'How to Play Football, QB Sneak. Backfield Spread,' *Lincoln Journal Star*, October 11, 1928.)

It was not until the Modern T formation emerged in 1940 that quarterbacks consistently put their hands under center for the hand-to-hand ball exchange. With the quarterback under center, the defense faces some uncertainty of whether the offense will run the sneak, but the deception and fakes that make the sneak sneaky disappear. Instead, it is a power play.

Field Judge

Though teams were slow to use the forward pass following its legalization, the 1906 rules also allowed the onside kick from scrimmage, effectively making punts recoverable by either team. The three-person officiating crews in place at the time had difficulty monitoring downfield passes and onside kicks, so the rule-makers added the **field judge** to watch things downfield in 1907. A 1910 rule prohibited passes more than twenty yards downfield putting more responsibility on the field judge. The rule-makers dropped that rule in 1912, and the field judge went with it, but the expanded use of the passing game led to the field judge rejoining the officiating crew in 1915.

Players and officials are spread around the field as Harvard executes a successful onside kick from scrimmage against Cornell. (1911 Cornell University *Cornellian*)

Goal Line Stand

Football has borrowed or adapted many terms from the military, including the reference to teams making a "stand," borrowed from the military's last stand. From the military's perspective, a "last stand" refers to a military unit defending a position against overwhelming odds, potentially sacrificing itself for the greater good. The last stand best known to

Americans was George Custer's, called Custer's Last Stand, within days of the event being reported.

While the implications of failure in football games are far less severe than in the military, writers began describing teams that successfully defended their goal line as making a **goal line stand**.

The term's first use described Harvard's defensive effort late in the second half of the 1905 Dartmouth game. After advancing to Harvard's 16-yard line, Dartmouth ran two plays that netted only one yard, after which they attempted and missed a field goal. Of course, few today would consider a defense stopping the offense at the 16-yard line as making a goal line stand, but if you invent a new term, you get to define its meaning.

The term next appears five years later, following Harvard's win over Williams, when a writer noted:

> Harvard showed its metal (sic) when it made that goal line stand against Amherst. Every game shows more reasons why there should be a really great team in the stadium a little later.[7]

That goal line stand came at the 3-yard line with one of the plays captured in the following image.

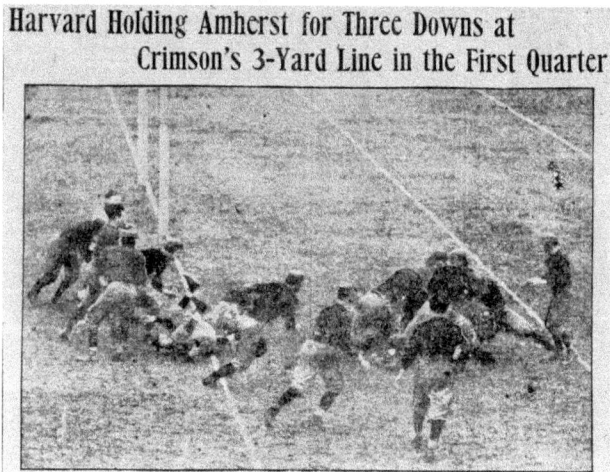

The second goal line stand referred to as a goal line stand.
('Harvard Holding Amherst For Three Downs At Crimson's 3-Yard Line In The First Quarter, 'Boston Globe, October 16, 1910.)

The following week Harvard played Williams, and the writer included the identical blurb as above, except he substituted Williams in place of Amherst.

"Goal line stand" appeared less than thirty times before 1920, several hundred times in the 1920s, and exploded in use in the 1930s.

Shoestring Tackle. Football originally required tackling ball carriers by the torso. Tackling above the knee became legal in 1888 and below the knee in 1903. The rule changes of 1906 helped open up offenses to some extent leading to more open-field tackles, some of which were described as **shoestring tackles**. However, a 1910 rule banned flying tackles, requiring tacklers to have at least one foot on the ground. The rule was seldom enforced and was eliminated in 1925.

Wind Sprints. Athletes in multiple sports sought to develop their wind or conditioning in the 1890s. Still, it was not until a Chicago lineman, Merrill Meigs, reported for practice out of shape in 1908 that **wind sprints** received mention after a particularly grueling practice.

4

THE NINETEEN TEENS

Tee

Early gridiron football used a rugby ball. Fatter and more rounded on the ends than today's football, a succession of modifications made the ball thinner, pointier, more aerodynamic, and easier to carry and throw.

While the impact of the reshaped ball on the forward pass is commonly understood, consider the impact of the reshaped ball on place kicks. A soccer ball set on the ground does not roll over because it is round, and early footballs, being closer to round, were also less prone to roll over. That allowed kickers to place the ball on the ground in a small divot made with the heel knowing the ball would remain standing for a place kick. As footballs became progressively pointier, however, balls required additional support to stay in place, so football borrowed an idea and term from golf.

Golf balls are round and, like soccer balls, do not fall over, but early golfers found them easier to hit and lift into the air when placed on a small mound of sand. Early golfers took the first stroke on each hole from within a circle, one club length from the last hole. The Scottish Gaelic word for circle is *taigh,* so the sand mounds became known as **tees**. Football kickers applied the same thinking and built dirt mounds scraped from grassless patches on the field. The first documented instance of a kicker using a tee came when Ewing Freeland, Vanderbilt's left tackle, did so in their 1910 game with Sewanee.

THE TWELVE THAT MADE OLD VANDY FAMOUS.

Left tackle Ewing Freehand was the first kicker known to use a tee. (1911 Vanderbilt University *Commodore*)

After Ewing, Auburn's Moon Ducote upped the ante by using his flimsy leather helmet as a tee in 1916, leading to a 1917 rule that made artificial tees illegal. Teams then stretched the definition of artificiality by using baked clay tees, which led to banning all tees in 1924. However, tees returned to college football in 1944 and have since been allowed or forbidden at times on kickoffs, field goals, and extra points.

"HORSE" HOBBS AND "BILL" CHURCH

Nevada's Bill Church shows his follow-through after kicking the ball from a dirt tee. (1923 University of Nevada, Reno *Artemisia*)

End Line and End Zone

Initially, the primary method of scoring a touchdown was to carry the ball across the goal line. When the forward pass became legal in 1906, a forward pass thrown or bouncing over the goal line was a turnover. The rules changed in 1912 to allow forward passes to cross the goal line, but the rule makers needed to limit how far behind the goal line players could legally catch a pass. They set the limit at ten yards, adding a stripe called the **end line**. The 1912 rule book designated the area between the goal line and the end line as the **end zone**.

Field Dimensions and Markings (1912-1926)

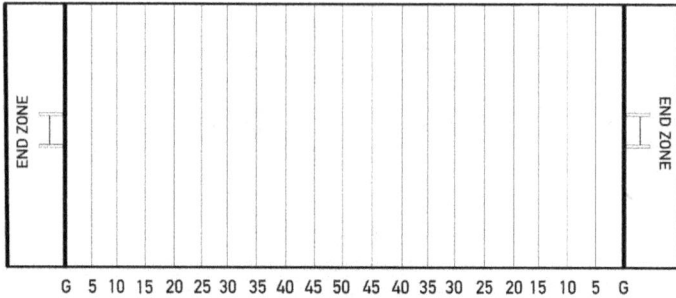

END ZONE

END ZONE

G 5 10 15 20 25 30 35 40 45 50 45 40 35 30 25 20 15 10 5 G

Adding two ten-yard end zones would have made the marked field twenty yards longer, too long for some stadiums. As a result, the rule makers eliminated the 55-yard line, making the marked field ten yards longer than it had been.

Tailback

The Traditional T formation designated one running back as the left half-back and another as the right halfback. Oddly, when the Notre Dame Box formation came on the scene in the first decade of the 1900s, and Pop Warner's Carlisle Tandem or Single Wing offense arrived in 1912, these position names remained unchanged.

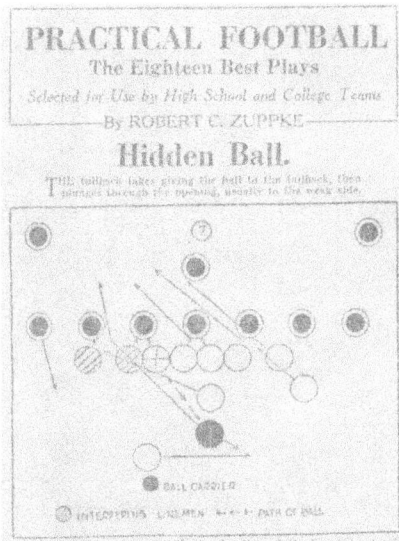

The play description mentioning the tailback is the first known use of
the term in print. (Zuppke, Robert C. 'Practical Football, The Eighteen
Best Plays, Hidden Ball,' *El Paso Herald*, October 20, 1925.)

Perhaps it was due to having Red Grange playing for him, but Bob
Zuppke was the first to distinguish the blocking halfback from the
running halfback when he called the runner, positioned deep or at the tail
end of the formation, the **tailback** in 1925. From that point on, "tailback"
referred to the deepest running back, sometimes including the fullback in
the Double Wing. The term was later adopted to refer to the deep back in
the I formation.

Nose for the Ball

"Having a nose for" described people with special or instinctive talents
well before Americans first played football. Though it took some time to
be applied to football, Huge Wagner, an All-American end at Pitt in 1913,
was the first player described as having a **nose for the ball** since he had a
good fortune or sixth sense to scoop up blocked punts and fumbles and
then race downfield for touchdowns. Wagner scored two defensive
touchdowns against Cornell in 1913 and did the same two weeks later
against Lafayette, falling on a blocked punt in the end zone and returning
a fumble fifty yards for a touchdown.

THE PLAY THAT MADE WAGNER FAMOUS

Huge Wagner prepares to scoop up a Lafayette fumble before rumbling 50 yards for
a touchdown at Forbes Field. (1915 University of Pittsburgh *Owl*)

Under Center and Hands Under Center

When football transitioned to the controlled scrimmage in 1882, centers
continued snapping with their feet to quarterbacks squatting a few feet
back. The quarterback's positioning was described as **under center** or
"under the center" in the mid-1910s, likely to differentiate it from their
alignment in the Single Wing or Notre Dame Box offenses.

Quarterbacks squatted directly behind or offset from the center but did not place
their hands in the center's crotch. (1908 Spalding's Official Foot Ball Guide)

With the introduction of the Modern T formation in 1940, quarterbacks stood immediately behind the center, placing their hands in the center's crotch, after which the center snapped the ball directly into the quarterback's hands. The T formation technique and positioning were referred to as "under center" or **hands under center**.

Flanker, Wide Receiver, and Split End

Other than the ends, the first position name for a player aligning wide was the **flanker**, which Stagg introduced a dozen years before the forward pass became legal. Stagg's original flanker was a halfback set fifteen yards outside the tackle and behind the line of scrimmage. Stagg's flanker often motioned back toward the formation to block the defensive end or tackle, like the crackback block of later years. Flankers also came in handy when running reverses.

Stagg undoubtedly borrowed "flanker" from the military, where "flanking" describes maneuvers around an enemy position. When the forward pass became legal in 1906, Stagg resurfaced the flanker, using them occasionally.

Players and teams to whom the ball was thrown or kicked have been called **receivers** since the mid-1910s. Receivers caught forward passes, punt receivers caught punts, and kicking teams booted the ball to the receiving team. Still, it was not until the early 1950s that **wide receivers** came to describe players who aligned wide.

Until the late 1920s, most offensive formations had the ends aligned within a foot or two of the tackles, so they were known simply as the left or right end. Then, teams began moving one or both ends one or two yards wider than usual. The tactic became known as the **split end**, though the players did not acquire that name because teams sometimes split their left end wide and sometimes the right end; neither specialized as a split end.

Kansas State's offense aligns in the Single Wing, with the right
end splitting several yards from the tackle. (1937 Kansas State
Royal Purple, Kansas State University Libraries)

Split end as a description of the position showed up in 1938 when the
University of the Pacific, then coached by the 76-year-old Amos Alonzo
Stagg, had an end line up fifteen or more yards wide of the tackle.

Flea Flicker and Hook and Lateral

The discussion regarding signals in the chapter on the 1890s covered the
progression from hand signals to short phrases, to numbers, and then to
word and number combinations to describe the formation, blocking
scheme, motion, routes, and the like. Bob Zuppke used a combination of
conventions, with most plays being numbered while trick plays received
names. For example, while coaching Oak Park High School near Chicago

around 1910, Zuppke had a player named Ghee, so he called a pass following a reverse the Ghee Haw. (Gee and Haw command draft horses to turn right or left.)

A second trick play had several variations, one coming on a fake field goal. Instead of snapping to the holder, the center snapped to the kicker, who threw a pass to the end. The end flipped the ball to the supposed holder, who had circled wide of the receiver. Zuppke explained in 1933 that a newspaper reporter who had seen Oak Park execute the play in 1911 remarked that the lateral resembled a monkey flicking a flea from its body, so the play became the **flea flicker**.

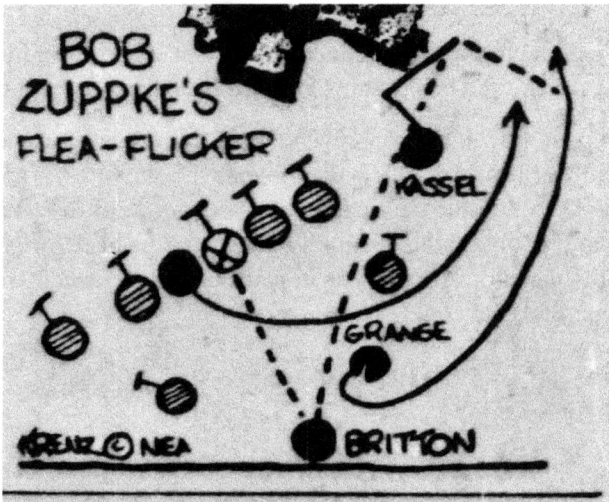

Red Grange was the holder and the recipient of the lateral on a twenty-yard touchdown run in the 1925 Illinois-Penn game. (Krenz, Art, 'Follow the Ball, *News Journal (Wilmington, DE)*, October 27, 1933.)

Although teams continued using the flea flicker, its use declined in the late 1930s. At the same time, teams paired the hook pass with a lateral to a second player, and this combination became known as the **hook and lateral.**

Flea flicker and hook and lateral were interchangeable until 1957 when Weeb Ewbank was looking for a new play while coaching the Baltimore Colts and recalled the flea flicker he used as a high school coach. Unfortunately, he misremembered the play or had run a different play at the high school level. Either way, Ewbank had the quarterback hand the ball to a back running up the middle. As the back neared the line, the back stopped and tossed the ball back to the quarterback, who threw a downfield pass. Since the Colts were a successful team at the time, and they called the play the flea flicker, others picked up the name, and Zuppke's "flea flicker" became associated with a different play.

Statue of Liberty

The paternity of some elements of football is difficult to trace, and that is the case with the **Statue of Liberty** play (aka the Cherry Picker). Some attribute its origins to Amos Alonzo Stagg, but he indicated that Fielding Yost fathered the play while coaching Ohio Wesleyan in 1897. That version of the story says the Statue of Liberty originated as a fake punt play in which the punter stood like the Statue of Liberty, holding the ball in the air as an end ran behind him, grabbed the ball, and swept the end

Others suggest Ray Morrison invented the play while quarterbacking Vanderbilt from 1908 to 1911. The problem with the Morrison version of the story is that multiple newspaper articles from 1913 to 1915 mention teams using the "old Statue of Liberty play." So Yost likely originated the play, but the name did not appear in print until 1913 when Geneva ran the play against Allegheny.

Trenches

It should be no surprise that one of the many military terms borrowed by football arrived in 1914. The war in Europe was only six weeks old and had not yet become bogged down in the trenches that characterized WWI. Nevertheless, trenches were first tied to football by Victor Ligda, coach of powerhouse Los Angeles Manual Arts, when he said that graduation had thrown bomb shells into other teams' football trenches.

Ligda's comment and others for the next thirty years used trenches to refer to teams in general. Perhaps due to parallels drawn between football's passing game and the role of air power in WWII, trenches became tied to linemen and line play immediately after WWII. Comments about the "battle in the trenches" and similar analogies became common and have grown more common over time.

Lateral and Flat Pass

Frank Hinkey was football's first four-time All-America while playing for Yale from 1891 to 1894. Like many alums of his time, Hinkey returned to Yale for a week or two in subsequent seasons to assist the team captain in preparing the team. However, times changed, and coaching became professionalized, leading the captain of Yale's 1914 team to hire Hinkey as the head coach.

Frank Hinkey and Tom Shevlin at Yale Field in 1914. (George Grantham Bain Collection, Library of Congress.)

Looking to innovate and make Yale's offense more explosive, Hinkey spent time in Canada consulting with Canadian rugby teams, who played a form of football blending elements of American football and rugby. To that point, Yale was known for power football, yet Hinkey installed plays with multiple players sweeping wide. When the ball carrier was about to be tackled, he passed the ball to a teammate running behind or parallel with him. Those passes became known as **laterals**. Interestingly, while the approach came from Canada, the term was not an import but home-grown. Over time, laterals became the generic term for backward passes, while "forward" dropped from forward pass, so we now use "pass" to describe a forward pass.

Despite the innovative laterals, Yale did not perform well under Hinkey, and the captain of the 1915 Yale team fired Hinkey toward the end of the season. Hinkey proved right about the need for offenses to stretch the field horizontally. Lateral passes became popular in the 1930s, likely influencing the development of option football that arrived in the 1940s.

Similarly, the desire to spread the field horizontally in the 1910s led to teams throwing **flat passes** as an alternative to downfield passing.

A Game of Inches

If only there were paternity tests for words and expressions attributed to multiple sports and parents. While some claim **a game of inches** first passed from Vince Lombardi's lips, others point to Branch Rickey, and another source suggests the term is associated with the game of horseshoes.

However, relying on newspapers for evidence takes us to Waco, Texas, in 1915, when Waco High led Austin High 6 to 3. At that point, an Austin player, Finley Henderson, drop-kicked a 46-yard field goal that barely went over the crossbar, causing the reporter to describe the day's events as **a game of inches**. The 1920s saw a handful of college games won or lost *by* inches.

From there, we head to Illinois, where an Illini assistant coach used the expression, "Football is a game of inches, not yards,[1]" in 1935 to describe the 1935 Notre Dame-Ohio State game he scouted. During the game, an Ohio State fumble brushed the fingertip of a hustling Notre Dame player before it went out of bounds. At the time, fumbles out of bounds went to the last team to touch the ball, not possess it. Soon after getting the ball, Notre Dame threw a long touchdown pass that launched another football expression, the "Hail Mary" pass.

"Game of inches" later appeared in a list of Bob Zuppke-isms compiled upon his retirement, so it may be that the assistant coach had repeated a Zuppke expression.

Blind Side or Blindside

There are few terms in sports with as varied a set of historical uses as **blind side**, though it had a consistent, core meaning. For example, blind side was used in the 1800s regarding boxers and horses with one functional eye. Also, rugby uses the expression to describe the side of the scrum closest to the sideline, while the role analogous to football's defensive end is the blindside flanker.

Blind side had two consistent uses in football before the mid-1950s. First, as with other sports, when teams were upset or nearly upset by a lesser team, the underdog was said to have snuck up on a team's blind side. The second meaning describes defensive players unexpectedly hit from the side on a trap or crackback block.

Blindsided, in current usage, typically describes a quarterback standing in the pocket who is hit from the backside by a pass rusher. Interestingly, the earliest reference to this form of being blindsided was not for a passer but to Harvard's All-American halfback Eddie Mahan who was pressured from the backside when punting against Princeton in 1915.

HEROES OF VICTORS AND FALLEN

Scovil, star of the Yale team in yesterday's rout, and Eddie Mahan, captain of the victorious Harvard eleven, said to be one of the greatest footballers that ever wore the moleskin.

Eddie Mahan follows through on a punt in an article published two weeks after being blindsided. ('Heroes of Victors and Fallen,' *San Francisco Examiner*, November 21, 1915.)

Describing quarterbacks as blindsided became common in the mid-1950s when Earl Morrall, Bobby Layne, and others became victims. The increased use of the term resulted from T formation quarterbacks dropping back and standing in the offensive backfield behind the relatively new pass-blocking scheme known as "pocket protection." The late 1950s and 1960s also saw increased analyses of the types of hits that led to injuries. These analyses ultimately led to outlawing of several forms of blindside hits (e.g., crackback, blocking below the waist on kicks).

Shock Troops

Early football did not allow substitutions and then allowed them only for injured players. A 1905 rule allowed substitutions at any time the ball was dead and formalized the convention that substituted players could not return to the game.

A side effect of players being unable to return to the game was that dazed or otherwise injured players often stayed on the field, taking time to recover before returning to play. Recognizing the rule created a safety threat, a 1910 rule allowed substituted players to return to the game at the beginning of a subsequent quarter. Coaches leveraged this rule after WWI by using **shock troops**, which initially meant swapping groups of substitutes, such as the four backs. However, the meaning shifted in 1924 when Knute Rockne started his second unit in the season opener to tire the opponent before inserting the first team. Rockne continued using his second team in this manner. Other teams with deep rosters followed suit.

Specialist and Special Teams

The combination of strict substitution rules and limited roster sizes affected how teams handled kickers, particularly kickers and punters who were not regular position players. Most teams had one position player act as the kicker and one or more position players who punted.

It took an innovator like Harvard coach, Percy Haughton, to recognize the opportunity and introduce **specialist** kickers to the game. Haughton used specialist kickers like baseball pinch hitters. For example, when Harvard had a field goal opportunity, the kicker substituted for player A who left the game until the next quarter. The kicker then attempted the field goal, ideally made it, remaining in the game to kickoff. Then, Player B subbed out the kicker following the kickoff.

When unlimited substitutions entered football in 1941, specialist kickers became common. But it was not until the late 1940s that coaches used separate platoons of players on kicks and punts and referred to them as **special teams**.

Special teams disappeared from the college game in 1953, returning in the mid-1960s when unlimited substitutions came back. By then, soccer-style kickers were changing from the occasional oddity to increasingly common due to their longer and more accurate kicks. During the same period, pro rosters expanded, allowing teams to carry specialist kickers. Special teams achieved sufficient importance by 1969 that the Los Angeles Rams hired Dick Vermeil and the Philadelphia Eagles hired Marv Levy as the NFL's first special teams coaches.

Coffin Corner Kick

Before the forward pass and other changes gave us modern football, football was a low-scoring field position game emphasizing punting. Superior punters were prized, and the ability to boot the ball contributed to more than one fullback and halfback gaining All-American honors.

Punting for distance had substantial value, but accuracy was also crucial, and periodic rule changes led to new punting strategies and new words to communicate those strategies. John Heisman suggested that punting to pin an opponent in the corner originated with Swarthmore and Penn player George Brooke, who played in the late 1880s and early 1890s. While teams today value punts that roll out of bounds close to the opponent's goal line, such punts had more value before hash marks arrived. Punts going out of bounds were spotted fifteen yards from the sideline, but punts stopping close to the sideline stayed there, and the return team started the possession from that spot. Imagine starting a possession on the one-yard line, one yard from the sideline. That would truly be a **coffin corner**, a term that first appeared in 1919. Although it is unclear how the name came into football, the term supposedly comes from the notches or insets in stairwell walls that provide clearance for longer items, including coffins to be carried up and down stairs.

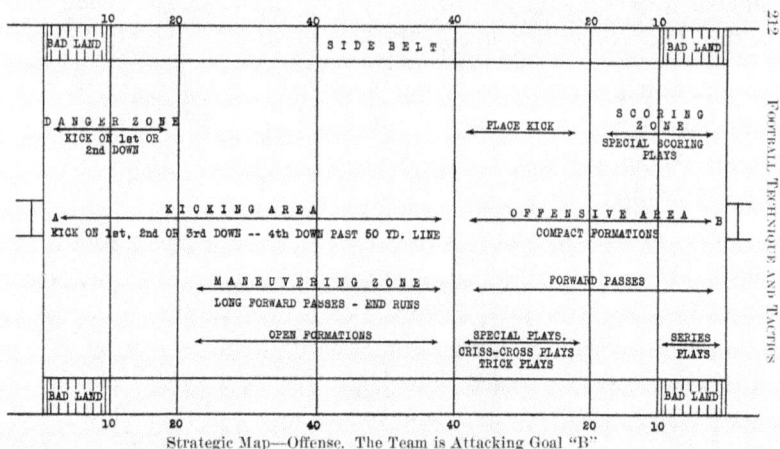

Strategic Map—Offense. The Team is Attacking Goal "B"

Illinois coach Bob Zuppke's strategic map did not use the coffin corner terminology but identified the areas as "Bad Land." (Zuppke, 1924)

Skeleton and Skelly Drills

Another term that football borrowed from the military is skeleton drill. During earlier times, when countries raised armies, regiments sometimes had their full complement of officers, but few enlisted personnel. These units were called skeleton regiments.

Since armies marched into battle in formation back then, officers needed to practice giving commands, so they placed the available troops at the corners of the formation, holding ropes to represent the formation's perimeter. Marching the rope-holding units around the parade grounds was known as skeleton drills.

The concept and terminology applied to football practice when teams had insufficient men or, more often, wanted to drill the backs separately from the linemen. For example, the University of Detroit used skeleton drills in 1915, as did Penn State, while preparing for the 1923 Rose Bowl. **Skeleton** or **skelly drills** became associated with the passing game as that part of the game developed.

Stickem Cloth or Strips

The vertical stripes and other patterns on the football jerseys of the 1910s to 1930s are iconic identifiers of the era, but they were initially used for their function, not form. **Stickem** (aka *stickum or friction*) **cloth or strips** began when ball carriers sewed rectangular or oval leather patches on the front of their jerseys and inner arms, thinking the ball would be less likely to slip from their grip. Vertical stripes and other designs replaced the large patches as the form became as important as the function. (Linemen, who did not carry the ball, began wearing them despite lacking a practical reason for doing so.)

Ohio State's 1916 team was an early adopter of stickem cloth. The players without friction strips may be linemen or substitutes. (1917 Ohio State *Makio*, The Ohio State University Libraries)

The strips fell into disuse as teams increasingly placed numbers on the front of their jerseys., though some teams had numbers and friction strips on their jersey fronts during the transition.

Washington State knocks an Oregon pass away from the receiver as friction strip uniforms take their dying breath. (1938 Oregon *Oregana*, University of Oregon Libraries)

Aerial Circus

Bands of troubadours, trapeze artists, and other circus performers once traveled from town to town, entertaining the locals. The same occurred when men left the surly bonds of earth in hot air balloons and aeroplanes. The traveling aerial circuses had parachutists drop from balloons and perform various tricks once planes could handle loops, barrel rolls, and wing walking.

Entertaining fans by moving the football through the air rather than the ground also became an **aerial circus**. The first known application to a football team came when Army Air Force planes staged an aerial circus over Birmingham's Rickwood Field as part of the festivities surrounding the 1918 Auburn-Vanderbilt game. So when Vanderbilt took to the air in their 21-0 victory, they also earned the aerial circus designation for their antics.

Notably, Vanderbilt's coach in 1918 was Ray Morrison, and the aerial circus appellation followed him as he moved between SMU and Vanderbilt in the 1920s and 1930s. Bucknell and Navy's offenses also earned the aerial circus description before the term became widely used in the 1930s.

· · ·

Basic Fundamentals

Before colleges had intramural programs, they often had class football teams with rosters filled by class members who were not varsity players. Class teams played one another, with some playing outside competition. The latter was the case when the University of Washington's junior class scheduled a game with the Tacoma Athletic Club in 1915. The Washington boys must have been serious about their team since the Tacoma Times indicated that:

> The juniors are being coached by "Conny" MacLean, former crack end of the University of Minnesota and Yale university (sic) elevens, and though with only two weeks practice behind them, the juniors have been well educated in all the intricacies and **basic fundamentals** of the famous Minnesota shift and the Yale forward pass.[2]

That appears to have been the first time someone used the expression publicly concerning football. Still, it was already in circulation in fields ranging from religion to engineering, and baseball and basketball coaches of the 1910s and 1920s talked of basic fundamentals well.

Under normal circumstances, that would be more than enough said about this topic since we have better things to do with our time than to discuss this inane expression. However, two short years later, none other than Walter Camp said:

> There is a sequence in development of attack that must be followed, first the basic and fundamental line attack, and then the fancy plays and frills. If the team has not the former, the latter will prove only a flash in the pan.[3]

While Walter did not say "basic fundamentals," he did say "basic and fundamental," which is equally offensive. And to think the Father of Football nearly fathered the most foolish of football expressions.

First, Second, Third, and Fourth Quarter. Football was a game of two halves until 1910. Looking to give players a short rest and allow injured players to be assessed, the game was split into 15-minute periods, which were immediately called quarters.

5

THE NINETEEN TWENTIES

Zone and Man-To-Man Defense

The strategies teams used to defend against the forward pass when it first became legal are unclear. Most teams ran defenses with six or seven-man lines, one or two players several yards behind the line, and two or three at various depths. Similarly, most offenses passed from tight formations, though some used their punt formations, with or without split ends.

By the late 1910s, however, coaches had borrowed both thinking and vocabulary from basketball by distinguishing between zone and man defenses. Eddie Casey, who played for Harvard in 1919 and coached Mount Union in 1920, was the first to be quoted distinguishing zone and man defenses.

> In the middle of the field, the best defense against the pass is the so-called **zone system**. Every backfield man on the defensive has a certain territory to protect.

> ...The short zones, which defend against the short passes, should be taken care of by the defensive fullback and the centre. The deep zones to protect against longer passes are covered by the two halfbacks. And an exceedingly long pass, which is a rarity now, is usually taken care of by the quarterback, which can come up from his position very quickly as he sees the play develop.

...Nearing the goal line of your own team, the defenders should change their positions from zone to individual-men defenders.[1]

The first mention of man-to-man defense came three years later when Ohio State played Illinois. The Buckeyes' use of man-to-man reflected their assigning two players to mirror Red Grange, following him wherever he went. It must not have worked too well, however, since Illinois won 9 to 0 to finish undefeated, for which they were later credited with a national championship. A few weeks later, Walter T. Scott, a football authority in Montana, used the term in the current sense when he argued coaches should use both man-to-man and territorial defenses, the latter being his term for zone defense.

Huddle and Snap Count

Calling signals at the line of scrimmage was consistent with the pace of play during football's first fifty years. Offenses lined up in the same formation play after play, spending little time between downs. The offense quickly lined up when one play ended, called the signals, and snapped the ball. The rapidity with which teams ran plays did not result from rules requiring teams to do so. Instead, it was a remnant of football's rugby origins.

Paul Hubbard, the quarterback at Gallaudet from 1892 to 1895, is credited with calling the first **huddle** in a game. Gallaudet, a university for the hearing impaired, used American Sign Language (ASL) to call signals because most games came against teams whose players were not hearing impaired and did not sign. However, Gallaudet played another squad in 1894 whose players understood ASL, so Hubbard had his team huddle before each play. Still, Yale's captain in 1898, Burr Chamberlain, appears to have been the first whose "huddle" proved worthy of mention in a story.

Despite some huddling in the nineteenth century, it was not until the 1920s that teams huddled consistently, following the lead set by Bob Zuppke's Illinois teams. Huddling simplified play-calling by eliminating the need for codes. It also ensured teammates heard the quarterback in the increasingly large and loud stadiums of the 1920s.

Illustration of offensive guards monitoring the ball when
snapping without a snap count. (Zuppke, 1924)

Another advantage of huddling was that defenses did not know how teams would align after leaving the huddle. While many offenses shifted just before the snap to gain an advantage, huddling teams ran up to the line, snapping the ball immediately and leaving defenses with little time to adjust to the offensive formation. Subsequent rule changes required players to pause at least one second after shifting or leaving the huddle.

Whether teams called signals at the line or huddled, quarterbacks communicated the upcoming play and the signal for the center to snap the ball, which became known as the **snap count** in the 1920s. Some signals called at the line were complicated, requiring players to add, subtract, or multiply to determine the snap count. Huddling allowed quarterbacks to directly communicate the play and snap count, leading to simple quarterback signals at the line.

Two-On-One, One-Two, and Double-Team Blocking

Many mass and momentum plays had the playside linemen block away from the hole as backside linemen and backs attacked the hole. When the rules changed to require seven men on the line of scrimmage, offenses needed new methods to open holes. One approach was to have two offensive linemen block one defender. However, it does not appear that a term immediately arose to describe two players blocking one. For example,

Pop Warner's play diagrams in *Football for Players and Coaches* (1912) instructed the tackle to help or assist the guard in blocking the defensive guard or tackle. Still, in the late 1920s, these blocks became known as **two-on-one blocks**, **one-two blocks** arrived in the mid-1930s, and **double-team blocks** came along in 1940, with the older terms remaining in use for some time.

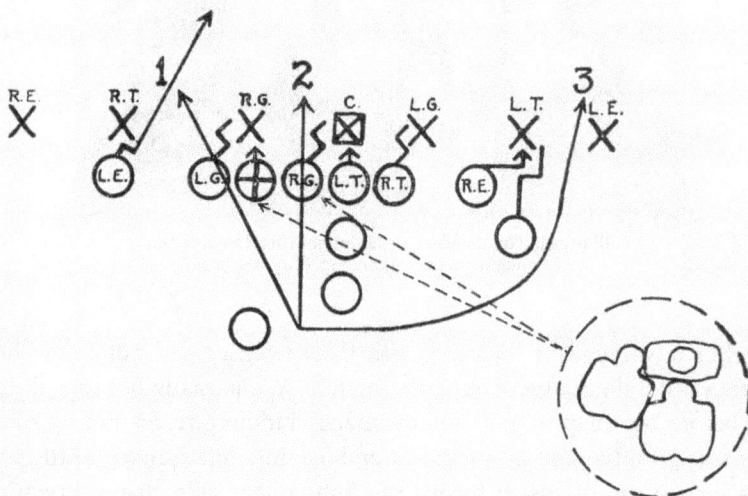

Diagram II.
Note "Key to Symbols of Charges and Blocks" on opposite page

The modern type of individual and "two on one" blocking is generally done with the main point of contact on the shoulders. However,

Two-on-one blocking as described and illustrated in Bunny Oakes' *Football Line Play* (1948).

Down Indicator or Box

A 1907 rule required the linesman to mark the line of scrimmage with an "iron rod." Some used unmarked rods about two feet long, and others used poles six feet tall topped with pennants. But having the linesman manage these markers meant they either left them in the ground while moving with the play, or they carried them along and lost an official marking of where the down originated.

The linesman stands on the field while holding a striped stick to mark the spot of the ball. (1926 Iowa State *Bomb*, Iowa State University Library Special Collections and University Archives)

During the same period, stadiums grew, making it more difficult for fans and scoreboard operators to track the spot of the play and the down. To address the problem, some clever soul developed the **down indicator**, commonly known as a **down box**. While it is unclear when they first appeared, it likely occurred in the late 1910s since a syndicated newspaper column about woodworking provided plans for a linesman's down indicator in 1922. The device was a simple box positioned atop a rod or pole with the numbers one through four painted on the box's panels. As the boxes grew larger and the poles taller, the down indicator was increasingly handled by a third chain gang member.

OREGON DRIVING THE BALL ACROSS PACIFIC'S FIVE-YARD LINE

A down box is in the lower right of the image. The side of the box with the numeral "1" faces the field, indicating that it is first down. (1926 Oregon *Oregana*, University of Oregon Libraries)

A host of improved down indicators came and went over the years. Inventors developed boxes displaying the current down on all four sides, poles with lights to indicate the down, the flip-type down box popular for decades, and the louvered version common today.

Offensive Line Coach

The name of the game's most crucial coaching position did not arrive until 1925. As reported at the time, after winning a national championship his senior season, former Notre Dame tackle Joe Dunn went to Atlanta in March to interview to be the **offensive line coach** at Georgia Tech. However, either he was not offered or did not accept the job since Tech hired an alum as the line coach instead.

The high honor of being the first to be called an offensive line coach went to Notre Dame's Joe Dunn. (1925 University of Notre Dame *Dome*)

Bootleg

Pop Warner's 1927 Stanford team ran variations of the Statue of Liberty throughout the year but saved a particular version for the Big Game with Cal. Leading 7-6 with the ball inside Cal's 10-yard line midway through the fourth quarter, Stanford ran what appeared to be a Statue of Liberty play from its Double Wing formation. Instead of giving the ball to the right wing sweeping left, Stanford's fullback, Biff Hoffman, kept the ball, concealed it on his hip, and ran around the right end for a touchdown. Called the "bootlegger" by Stanford's players, they shortened the name to **bootleg.** Plays with a fake handoff followed by rolling opposite the run action have since become standard.

Interestingly, Stanford's bootleg and other backfield trickery upset Eastern sportswriters when used against Army in 1928. One Eastern writer argued that Stanford's tricky ball handling was unsportsmanlike and should be outlawed:

> ...we shall have to draw some kind of line marking off where deception ends and gross fraud begins. I am thinking particularly of some the Stanford plays which had all the earmarks of petty larceny, second-story work and obtaining yardage under false pretenses. I saw those Stanford halfbacks do things with the football that no person of high moral principles would countenance.[2]

As occurred many times in football history, tactics viewed as unsportsmanlike and contemptible during one era become quite ordinary later on.

Flag Route and Corner Route

The goal posts stood on the goal line of American football fields until 1927, when they shifted to the end line. (The NFL returned the goal posts to the goal line in 1933 when they stopped using the NCAA rule book.) With the move to the end line, there was concern that players and fans would mistake the end line and the goal line. That led groundskeepers at many stadiums to paint the end zones with stripes, checkerboards, and other decorations that did not exist previously. In addition, some stadiums added yardage numbers or placed flags at the goal line and sideline intersection.

A flag and sign mark the intersection of the goal line and sideline at Iowa State. (1946 Iowa State *Bomb*, Iowa State University Library Special Collections and University Archives)

The flags quickly became an aiming point for long and short passes thrown to those spots, so routes pointed to that spot became **flag routes**. Others called them "coffin-corner passes," but after WWII, they dropped "coffin" from the name, and it became known as the **corner pass**.

Bomb

The long line of military terms adopted by football continued in 1929 when Tennessee's Peabody High upset Nashville Central High via a touchdown pass. Described as a "long aerial bomb,[3]" the pass traveled 15 yards in the air before the catch and tackle. Luckily for the offense, the defender did not keep the receiver in his grasp, so the receiver got up and ran it in for the touchdown. (The high schools followed NCAA rules at the time, and the "in the grasp" portion of the dead ball rule remained in effect until 1932.)

For the next thirty years, **bomb** saw occasional use as a substitute for a long pass and was nearly always preceded by descriptors such as "long aerial "or "long distance." In the early 1960s, however, writers began referring to these passes as long bombs or simply as bombs.

X's and O's

While it is unclear who first diagrammed a football play, we know that Princeton captain Edgar Allen Poe (the writer's second cousin, twice removed) used checkers to illustrate plays for his teammates in 1889. The newspaper reporter who told that story included two play diagrams in the article, using circles (or the letter O) for the offense and shaded circles for the defense.

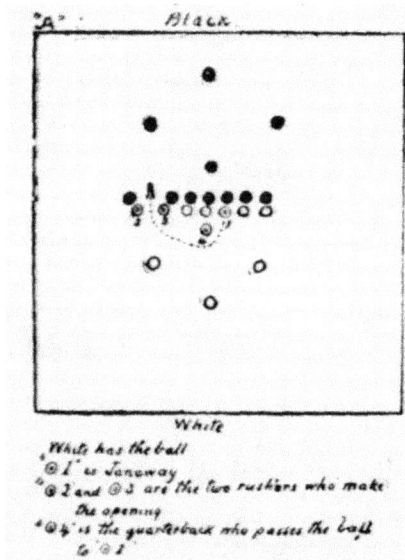

One of Edgar Allen Poe's checkered play designs had the right guard pulling behind the quarterback and running off tackle left. ('Checkerboard Football,' *Evening Star (Washington, D. C.)*, December 14, 1889.)

Stagg and Williams also used circles for the offense and defense in their 1893 book, but they filled in the circles representing the offense. Camp and Deland's 1896 *Football* used little figures, while Pop Warner used little figures or empty circles, depending on the book.

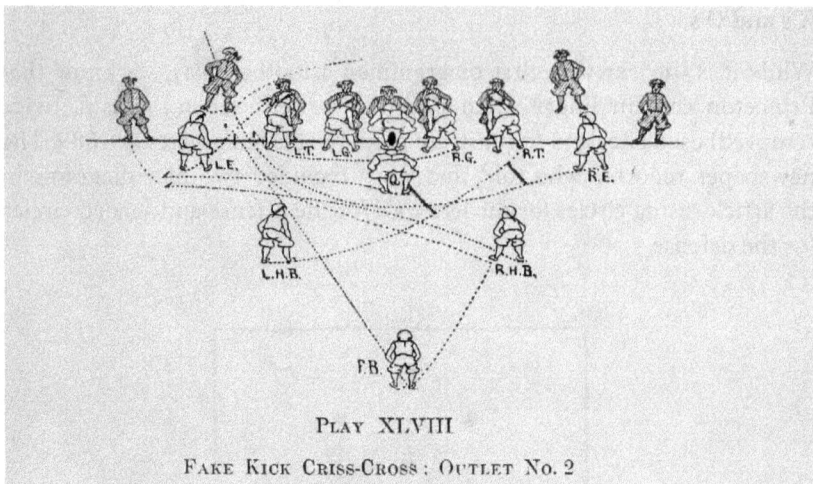

PLAY XLVIII

FAKE KICK CRISS-CROSS: OUTLET No. 2

Walter Camp had many good and several bad ideas, as demonstrated by his use of
silly little figures in play diagrams. (Camp and Deland, 1896.)

There may have been others, but the first coach known to use X's for the
offense and O's for the defense was Army's Charles Daly, as he did in his
1919 book, *American Football.*

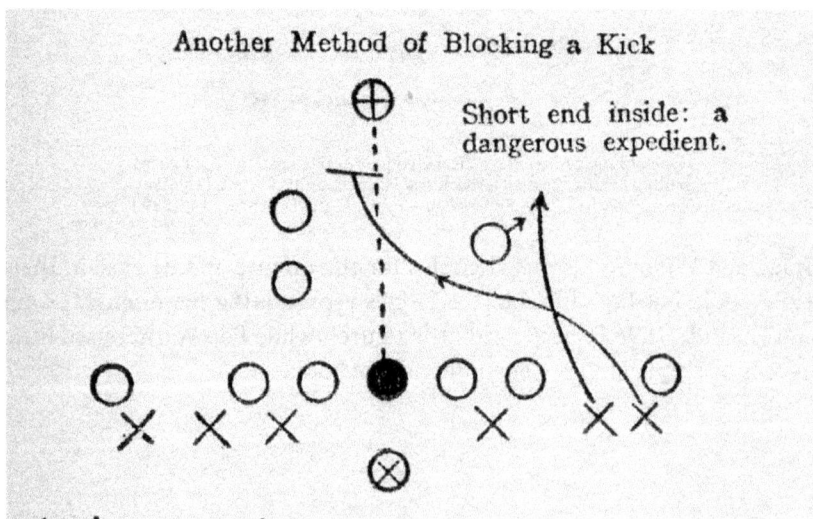

Another Method of Blocking a Kick

Short end inside: a
dangerous expedient.

Unlike others of the era, Daly used X's and O's in his play diagrams. (Daly, 1919)

Daly may not have originated the expression -it first appeared in print in a 1927 article concerning Pop Warner- but the expression caught on, and its use has spread well beyond the football field.

Clipping

Football has always been a rough and, at times, dirty game. The elimination of the flying wedge, outlawing multiple men in motion, and requiring seven men on the line of scrimmage targeted various aspects of mass plays. Other safety-oriented efforts focused on individual players, barring punching, kicking, tripping, piling on, and similar acts.

One element of dirty play that took a while to ban was hamstringing or cutting down, which originally meant severing or **clipping** a leg tendon. Hamstringing occurred when players rolled into the lower back legs of opponents not directly involved in a play (e.g., someone well behind a downfield play).

CLIPPING FROM BEHIND

PENALTY—15 YDS. FROM SPOT OF THE FOUL

('Clipping From Behind,' *Sioux City Journal*, October 29, 1923.)

Calls to outlaw hamstringing were unsuccessful until George Foster Sanford, the Rutgers coach, argued against it during a 1920 rules interpretation meeting. Others present, including Princeton assistant coach Frank Glick, argued that hamstringing was a part of football and should be retained. At the time, Sanford was 52 years old and challenged anyone at the event to allow him to demonstrate hamstringing on them as he would surely break their leg. At 27 years old, Glick took the challenge, and Sanford hamstrung him in front of the crowd. Though Glick's leg did not break, he lost the floor vote, and hamstringing became illegal in college football.

The rule did not prohibit clipping *per se*. Instead, it fell under the unsportsmanlike category as "unnecessarily running into a player obviously out of the play even before the ball has been declared dead.[4]" It did not address striking an opponent from behind, only hitting someone not involved in the play.

A 1925 rule made clipping a 25-yard penalty rather than a 15-yard penalty, which had the unintended effect of making some officials reluctant to call the penalty. However, continued pressure to expand the definition of clipping led to a 1933 rule making it illegal to strike from behind an opponent not carrying the ball while also reducing the penalty to 15 yards.

Gang Tackle and Oskie

Modern English received the word gang from an Old Norse word that described a journey, especially one taken with others. The term was applied later to work groups and tools, often those involving manual labor.

Gang tackle and gang tackling, which describes when two or more defenders tackle the ball carrier, first appeared in 1913 in an article describing Nebraska's defense in wins over Kansas and Minnesota. It appeared again in a *Los Angeles Times* article about Washington & Jefferson's defense in their 1922 Rose Bowl tie with California.

While its use predates Bob Neyland's arrival as head coach at Tennessee in 1926, he was responsible for popularizing the term. Besides winning four national championships at Tennessee, Neyland is remembered today for preaching seven maxims that defined winning football. He wrote the maxims on blackboards and had his team recite them before games. (Tennessee fans recite them before games to this day.)

HOLM STOPPED BY FINNEY, HUG, AND SAUNDERS.

Tennessee defenders Finney, Hug, and Saunders gang tackle Alabama's All-America
quarterback Tony Holm in a 1929 game. (*The Volunteer*, 1930. Yearbook of the
University of Tennessee, Knoxville, University of Tennessee, Knoxville – Libraries)

Neyland's fifth maxim was:

> Ball, oskie, cover, block, cut and slice, pursue and gang tackle for this is the
> WINNING EDGE.[5]

Although it is unclear when Neyland first preached gang tackling to his
Volunteers, several 1928 articles mention Tennessee's gang tackling, and
reports from the 1930s commonly tie gang tackling to Tennessee.

The second word in Neyland's fifth maxim also has ties to Neyland and
Tennessee. According to Herc Alley, Tennessee's right end in 1928,
Neyland insisted that Tennessee defenders yell "Oskie Wow Wow" after
making an interception or causing a fumble so teammates could hustle to
the ball or block a player wearing the opposite color. (A University of
Tennessee reference site suggests Neyland borrowed the term from Illinois and their marching band tune, "Oskee Wow Wow," published in
1911.)

Yelling "Oskie Wow Wow" remained a Tennessee-only practice until
Volunteer alum and Georgia Tech coach, Bobby Dodd, had his 1950 team
yell it after making an interception, though not a fumble. By 1957, Bill
Elias, Purdue's secondary coach, applied it to interceptions as well but
dropped the "Wow Wow," From that point, Oskie spread and became the
go-to post-interception word nationwide.

. . .

Game Clock and Play Clock

The game clock and play clock are understood to be separate tools today, but their origins are intertwined. Neither term existed in early football since timekeeping was the responsibility of one official who used a watch or stopwatch to track the time and periodically inform the team captains of the time remaining in the period.

However, folks in several locations had the idea to place a large clock or similar device on the scoreboard visible to players, coaches, and fans. The idea became a reality when an engineering professor at Wisconsin created the first "Time to Play Clock" in 1926, which the Badgers used for football and basketball games. For football games, a timekeeper on the sideline monitored the field judge, starting and stopping the scoreboard clock based on the field judge's actions.

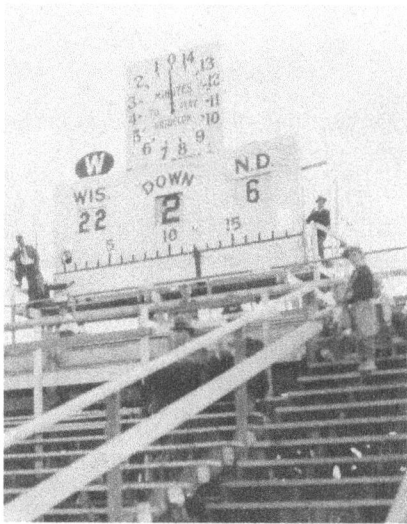

The "Time to Play Clock" was installed atop the scoreboard at Camp Randall in 1928. (University of Wisconsin Libraries)

After installing these clocks, people mentioned the "clock" when speaking of the time left in the game and "scoreboard clock" for the physical clock. However, that began changing in the 1930s when Herb Dana, a West Coast referee, wrote about the specific situations that cause the **game clock** to stop. Others picked up on "game clock," which soon referred to both the conceptual time left in the game and the physical clock.

When teams began shuttling players in and out of the game with the onset of two-platoon football in the 1940s, Jimmy Phelan, the coach at St. Mary's, argued for adding large **play clocks** in the stadium to help quarterbacks keep on track. However, nothing came of the idea until 1976, when the NFL installed large clocks at either end of the field to assist quarterbacks in avoiding delay of game penalties.

Single Wing

Few offensive innovations have impacted football as much as Pop Warner's Single Wing, which became the game's dominant offense for over thirty years. Its sibling, the Double Wing, was the first popular one-back offense after Stanford used it to win the 1926 national championship. As important, many of their underlying principles continue in use today.

Single Wing

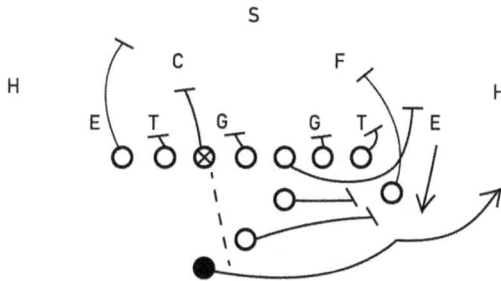

Illustration of a sweep from the Single Wing. The center snaps the ball directly to the tailback, leading him as he begins running to the right. (Adapted from Warner, A Course in Football for Players and Coaches, 1912)

Interestingly, elements of what became known as the Single Wing were part of Pop Warner's end back and Carlisle Formation beginning in 1907. Still, it was not until a 1912 rule change allowing the player receiving the snap to run right, left, or up the middle that the Single Wing took off. That also happened to be Jim Thorpe's senior year, and his ability to run, pass, and kick the ball made him the original triple threat.

Warner referred to the Single Wing as Formation A and the Double Wing as Formation B in his 1927 book, *Football for Coaches and Players*. **Single**

Wing arrived on the scene in 1928 when Bill Roper, then Princeton's coach, used the term to differentiate the Single Wing from the Double Wing, which Warner introduced several years earlier.

6

THE NINETEEN THIRTIES

Shovel Pass

The **shovel pass** stands among the football terms with the murkiest beginnings. Some say it arrived when Walter "Bug" Bujkowski threw an improvised shovel pass for the NFL's Duluth Eskimos in 1927. Unfortunately for Bug, his name does not appear on the Eskimos' 1927 team roster, period newspapers, or current football sources. Instead, he only appears on two blog sites that tout his purported feat.

Another incorrect claim says Western Maryland's Stoney Willis first shoveled a pass when he tossed a pair of underhanded, behind-the-line-of-scrimmage passes to teammate Jimmy Dunn, who took them 30 and 39 yards for touchdowns when Western Maryland tied Boston College in 1932. Utah coach "Cactus" Jack Curtice also receives credit for pioneering the shovel pass in some 1950s sources.

Unfortunately, for all three, none were present at the first shoveling. Instead, the **shovel pass** first appeared in 1930 after Wisconsin executed one against Illinois, and Minnesota did the same versus Northwestern the same weekend. Although "shovel pass" made its debut that weekend, the coverage suggests it was already as old as dirt, perhaps due to others having thrown screen passes or other behind-the-line-of-scrimmage passes. However, the distinctive element of the early shovel pass was that it was an underhand throw; hence, the shovel in its name.

· · ·

Button Hook, Hook, Curl, and Comeback

No one had thrown a legal forward pass before 1906, so each team that took the opportunity created their passing attack from scratch. As a result, many passed the ball in ways that did not stand the test of time, while a few techniques remained part of the game. St. Louis University threw the first legal forward pass and had the most sophisticated attack of 1906, but even their approach had elements that now seem strange.

The Billikens pioneered the overhand spiral pass that became standard, threw from their punt formation (akin to today's shotgun formation), and often tossed double-digit passes per game. Like everyone else, they had to figure out where to send their eligible receivers and when to throw them the ball. That all seems obvious today, but we benefit from nearly 120 years of experience with the forward pass. They had none.

St. Louis U's solution was to send their receivers straight downfield and to turn around when the quarterback yelled, "Hike." Using verbal commands to alter receiver routes did not remain in the game long, but the Billikens were undefeated in 1906, so it worked for them. The important point for this discussion is that their receivers were the first to run downfield, turn around, and look for the ball at that spot.

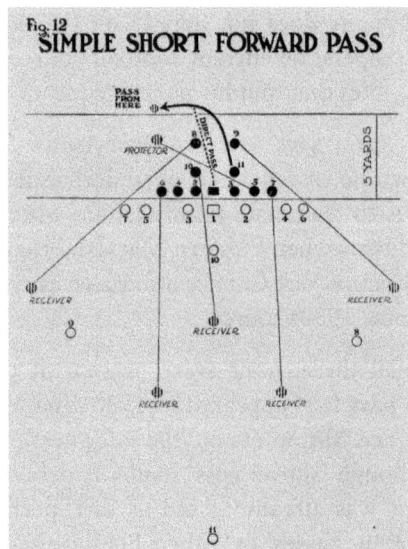

On this early pass play, the quarterback goes in motion to receive a direct snap and throws from five yards behind the line of scrimmage. The receivers turn around after the quarterback yells, "Hike." (Reed, 1913)

Gus Dorais and Knute Rockne receive credit for developing a similar route in 1913. Their innovation had Rockne, an end, run to a certain depth before turning around and taking a few steps back toward his quarterback, Dorais, who had already thrown the ball. Presumably, they had a name for the route, but it is unknown.

Knute Rockne was the left end for Notre Dame's 1913 football team. Quarterback Gus Dorais stands behind the left guard. (1913 University of Notre Dame *Dome*)

In the early 1930s, this route became known as a **hook** or **button hook**, following the Victorian-era hooked tool used to pull buttons through buttonholes on clothing and shoes. The general route became known as the **curl** by the early 1950s and the **comeback** in the late 1950s.

Hail Mary Pass

Among the more colorful terms for a pass play is the **Hail Mary**, which now describes a long, last-minute pass thrown by teams trailing on the scoreboard. But it was not always so, and if you believe the story, the original Hail Mary was not a pass play.

The legend of the Hail Mary play began in 1932 when one of Notre Dame's Four Horsemen, Jim Crowley, spoke at the American Football Coaches Association banquet. Crowley told the crowd of Notre Dame's come-from-behind victory over Georgia Tech in 1922. Georgia Tech twice fumbled deep, and when Notre Dame failed to move the ball, a lineman, who happened to be Presbyterian, suggested the team say a Hail Mary in the huddle before the fourth-down play. Notre Dame scored on a running play, and a legend was born. Of course, the legend may be only a legend since there was no public mention of the Hail Mary incident until Crowley's speech almost ten years later.

An action shot from the 1922 Notre Dame-Georgia Tech game,
which the Irish won 13-3. (1923 Notre Dame *Dome*)

The Hail Mary resurfaced in 1935 when Irish quarterback, William Shakespeare, threw long desperation passes to beat Ohio State and tie Army. It also popped up during the lead-up to Georgetown, another Catholic school, playing Mississippi State in the 1940 Orange Bowl.

Notre Dame's William Shakespeare punted, ran, and passed the ball in their victory
at Ohio Stadium. (1936 Ohio State Makio, The Ohio State University Libraries)

The Hail Mary pass escaped its Catholic origins in the late 1950s and early 1960s, being mentioned in isolated instances from coast-to-coast. It exploded on the football scene following Navy's 1963 victory over Michigan, when Heisman Trophy-winning quarterback Roger Staubach described his last-minute pass as a "Hail Mary" in his post-game comments.

Since then, the term has described many throws, most famously by another Heisman winner, Doug Flutie, whose scrambling last-second bomb to beat Miami in 1984 cemented the Hail Mary in football consciousness.

Redshirt, Redshirting, Scout Team, and Walk-On

Returning to the earlier discussion of scrub teams, some scrub teams wore whatever equipment was available, while others wore coordinated attire. For example, Harvard's scrubs wore black jerseys as early as 1908, while Cornell's 1917 scrub team wore red jerseys, leading to them being called **redshirts.**

Of course, scrub or redshirt team members could move up to varsity status. Depending on the conference or school eligibility standards, their time spent as a redshirt did not count toward their years of eligibility. Redshirting took a step toward its modern meaning in 1936 due to Warren Alfson of Nebraska, a backup sophomore guard who had not played in a game by mid-season. Rather than potentially be inserted late in one or two games, Alfson asked to spend the rest of the season with the redshirts, thereby retaining his year of eligibility. As the first known example of **redshirting**, Alfson became a three-year starter and senior All-America on Nebraska's 1941 Rose Bowl team. (Southern schools often referred to their scrub teams as "bohunks," so redshirting was called bohunking in the South into the late 1950s.)

Nebraska's Vike Francis scores against Stanford in the 1941 Rose Bowl as Warren Alfson (#22) looks on. ('Stanford Wins Over Nebraska,' *Pasadena Post*, January 2, 1941)

By the time Alfson played at Nebraska, major college rosters had expanded the scouting of future opponents. Assistant coaches, who missed their team's games to scout opponents, then spent the next week leading the third and fourth team players in mimicking the upcoming opponent in practice. Having introduced the world to redshirting, it is notable that Nebraska also had the first documented use of the term, **scout team**.

A similar issue concerns the difference between players on college teams who receive football scholarships and those who do not. SEC schools were the first to award formal athletic scholarships in the 1930s. The Big Ten officially allowed full-ride athletics scholarships in the early 1960s, leading Woody Hayes of Ohio State and Alex Agase of Northwestern to refer to players who tried out for the football team without benefit from a scholarship as **walk-ons**. Presumably, they borrowed the term from the dramatic world where actors with minor, typically non-speaking roles, were called walk-ons.

Scrimmage Vest

The original redshirts distinguished the offense from the defense in practice. It is unclear whether Cornell's scrubs always wore red jerseys while the varsity wore another color or whether the scrubs slipped a red vest over their jerseys. Of course, similar problems faced Cornell and other teams on game day since, like most, they had one set of jerseys and wore them for every game, even when they shared team colors with their opponent. The Cornell Big Red solved this problem by wearing white vests over their jerseys when playing teams like the Colgate Red Raiders. (Now, just the Raiders.) Period photographs show other teams doing the same for games during the early 1920s.

Cornell, on defense, wears white vests with numbers on the back during their 1921 game with Colgate. (1922 Cornell University *Cornellian*)

At least some teams of the era wore vests during practice, though doing so goes unmentioned in the newspapers.

Smith Gains on the Scrubs

Wisconsin wore vests in practice during the 1919 season. (1920 Wisconsin *Badger*, University of Wisconsin Libraries)

The first mention of such gear in print came in the mid-1940s when various high schools placed bids for football equipment in local newspapers, including **scrimmage vests**. Sometimes called *practice vests*, their blousy appearance resembled pinafores, so they also were called *pinnies* or *pennies*.

Straight On, Straight-Ahead, Conventional and Soccer-Style Kicker

Which came first, the "soccer-style kicker" or the "straight-ahead kicker?" As you might suspect, the answer depends on whether the question concerns the technique or the terminology.

Regarding the technique, football kickers used the **straight-ahead**, **straight-on**, or **conventional** method almost exclusively until the 1960s. The straight-ahead approach dominated gridiron football, earning its name only after an alternate technique gained attention. Still, **soccer-style kickers** and the term were around longer than most fans recognize.

The first kicker believed to employ the soccer-style technique was Jack Pence, a drop kicker for Coe College in the early 1920s. He was best known for kicking a 59-yard field goal against Drake in 1923, then the third-longest drop-kicked field goal on record. He had five other drop-kicked field goals exceeding forty yards. Pence kicked the ball with his instep, but his technique was not described as soccer-style until decades later.

The first kicker described as kicking soccer style was a soldier named Gardner, who kicked for the 21st Infantry team in Hawaii in 1933. Others described as soccer-style kickers included Gene Silberberg of Benedictine College in Kansas in the late 1940s and a handful of other small college players. Among those kicking soccer-style at higher levels of football was Paul Douglas, who did so for Illinois in the late 1940s and early 1950s and kicked in an exhibition game for the New York Giants in 1953. Similarly, Jim Fraser kicked soccer-style for Wisconsin in the late 1950s and played for the Hamilton Tiger-Cats in 1961. He also kicked several extra points for the Denver Broncos in 1962 and led the AFL in punting average in 1962, 1963, and 1964.

So, soccer-style kickers were around and described as sidewinders long before Pete Gogolak arrived at Cornell in 1961. Nevertheless, it was not until Gogolak came on the scene that several terms for the conventional kicking approach came into use.

Coe's Jack Pence prepares to drop kick. (Coe College Hall of Fame)

Side Zones, Inbound Lines, Hash Marks, Lockney Lines, and Yard-Line Extensions

In football's early days, teams had five options to bring the ball back into the playing field after it went out of bounds. Rule changes took four options away by 1904, and the ball has been moved onto the field at varying distances from the sideline since then.

However, when a play ended within the field of play, the next play started at that spot -whether it was an inch, a foot, or any other distance from the sideline. Teams often started plays with the center and quarterback against the sideline and their teammates positioned infield from them.

Montana set to run a play with a helmetless Single Wing guard aligned next to the sideline. (1927 Idaho *Gem of the Mountains, University of Idaho Yearbook, Vol. 24, University of Idaho Library Special Collections and Archives, Moscow, ID.)*

Both the NFL and NCAA changed the inbounding rule in 1933. The 1933 NFL rule book called the area between the sideline and ten yards infield the **side zone**, while the NCAA did not name the space. The NCAA's 1933 rule book includes a diagram showing a properly marked field with stripes intersecting the yard lines ten yards from the sideline, but the NCAA did not label those stripes until 1947 when they called them **inbound lines**. (Various high school rule-making bodies referred to the stripes as inbound lines starting in 1934.)

Reporters occasionally referred to the stripes as inbound lines before the NCAA adopted the term in 1947, but **hash mark** did not enter the picture until a reporter used it to describe the location of a 1947 Baylor field goal attempt. Its next use came in 1950. (Hash marks had long been slang for stripes on the sleeves of military uniforms that indicated the wearer's number of tours or enlistments.)

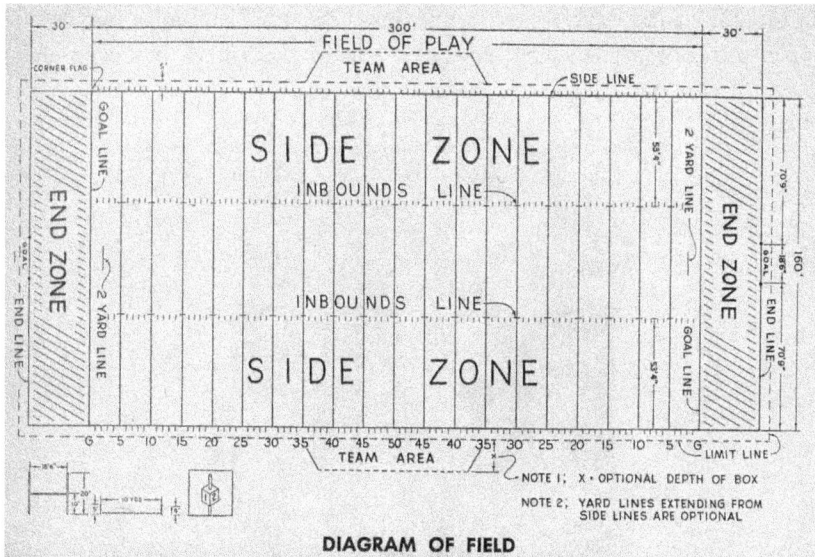

The 1957 NCAA rule book was the first to show both inbound lines and Lockney Lines. (1957 Official NCAA Football Guide)

Of course, the inbound lines or hash marks intersect the yard lines, and another set of lines joined them in 1954. Invented by an everyday fan, John Lockney, **Lockney Lines** are the short stripes running parallel to the yard lines that appear near the hash marks and the sidelines on each yard line, not ending with a 0 or 5. Unfortunately, the NCAA calls them "short yard-line extensions," a term so bureaucratically unfriendly that it has not appeared in a newspaper.

Horse-Collar Tackle

Horse-collar tackles can cause leg and other injuries when the ball carrier twists awkwardly while being tackled. While uncommon, a series of severe injuries during the 2004 season led the NFL to ban horse-collar tackles the next year. The NCAA followed suit in 2008, as did the high schools in 2009.

Ironically, grabbing the back of the shoulder pads was not called a horse-collar tackle until the early 1940s, and it was not due to a lack of familiarity with horse tack. Instead, it was due to the absence or flimsiness of shoulder pads before the mid-1920s.

In football's early days, no one wore shoulder pads. Soft pads sewn on the jersey exterior arrived in the second half of the 1890s, but even then, many did not pad their upper bodies.

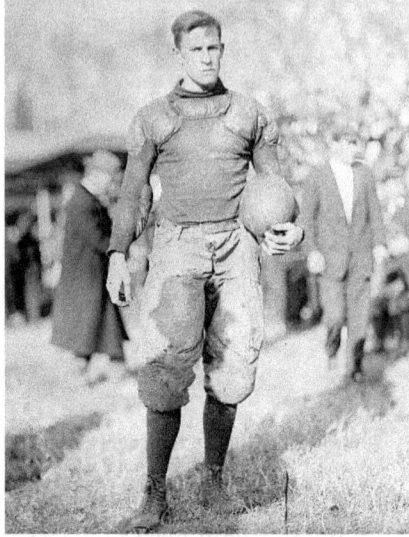

The exterior shoulder and chest pads worn by this Georgetown player were typical of the pre-WWI era. (Harris & Ewing, 1911, Library of Congress)

By the 1920s, almost every player wore shoulder pads with a single level of leather, fiber, and felt pads, generally kept in place by straps around the upper arms. Their light construction and loose fit meant that even when tacklers grabbed runners by the back of the shoulder pads, they did not gain the leverage until the tighter-fitting, cantilevered pads came on the market in the 1920s. Once more substantive shoulder pads appeared on the field, so did horse-collar tackles.

FOOT BALL SHOULDER PADS

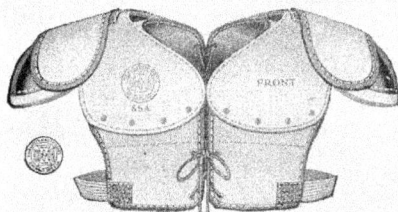

Scholastic Model SSA

A light weight pad especially designed for high and prep school use. The shoulder protection is of solid fibre arched over a foundation of white canvas which distributes the blow over the entire pad without reaching the body. The shoulder caps are made of solid molded leather padded with white felt. Additional protection of molded fibre faced with pebbled cowhide over shoulder joint.

No. SSA

Wide elastic chest strap. Shoulder caps, shoulder joints and chest protection strongly stitched in place and reinforced with rivets.

Retail Price $9.00

School Price $6.00

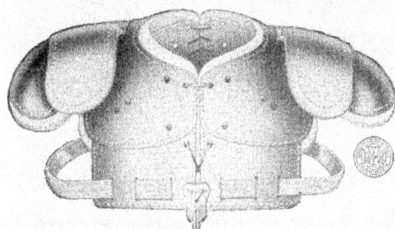

No. 37—Solid tan strap leather padded with heavy white felt and reinforced with fibre over chest. Molded and stiffened leather shoulder caps. Shoulder joint protection of solid fibre faced with pebbled cowhide. Adjustable elastic around chest holds pad firmly in place and eliminates straps under arms. Shoulder caps and shoulder joint protection stitched and riveted in place. Perforated for ventilation, "Jiffy" lacing.

Retail Price.............$8.50

School Price........$5.40

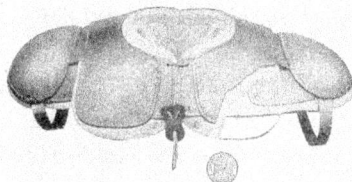

No. 37

No. 31—The chief feature is the double thickness of white felt padding faced with solid tan strap leather which completely covers the chest and collar bones. Additional solid strap leather protection over shoulder joint. Shoulder caps are molded and stiffened strap leather. Light in weight, yet gives full protection. Elastic bands. Fitted with "Jiffy" quick lacing device.

Retail Price $6.50

School Price $4.35

No. 31

Shoulder pads of the early 1920s resembled the bottom set, while more substantial cantilevered sets like the top two arrived later in the decade. (1929-30 Athletic Supply Company catalog)

The top two sets of shoulder pads are more substantial and strap around the chest, creating leverage when grabbed from behind.

Squib Kick

We discussed coffin-corner punts earlier, but punting strategies changed with the introduction of hash marks in 1933. Coffin corner punts that went out of bounds or stopped close to the sidelines were now moved to the hash marks ten yards infield. Since punters could no longer pin opponents in the corner, teams took the easier path and concentrated on pinning them inside the 10-yard line. Teams pinned deep often punted on first or second down to escape trouble, making for boring football.

With the hash marks ten yards infield (obscured by a white-jerseyed player on the 5-yard line), teams still were cornered at times. (1935 Georgia Tech *Blue Print*)

The situation led to a 1941 rule in which players on the punting team touching the ball inside the ten-yard line resulted in a touchback, which kept the punt coverage players from stopping balls rolling toward the end zone.

The rule had more impact on teams with less skilled punters, and Red Sanders must have considered his 1942 Vanderbilt team to be one of them. Rather than attempt to drop the ball inside the 10-yard line, Sanders instructed his punters to have the ball roll dead inside the 20-yard line. Since these punts often came when Vanderbilt was already in the opponent's territory, they were short punts, earning the name **squib kicks**. (Squibs are small firecrackers or short passages of writing.)

Second Guesser, and Grandstand, Armchair, and Monday Morning Quarterbacks

Football requires an ongoing stream of decisions. What is the best strategy for this game? Which play should we run next? To which receiver should we throw the ball? Regardless of who made those and other decisions, some fans question the strategies and happily let others know their opinions. Of course, quarterbacks and coaches are not always right, but those who consistently question their decisions are never wrong.

One of our terms for such people goes back to Victorian England when newspapers had contests where participants submitted answers to puzzles or predicted the scores of athletic events. Similar contests occurred in the U.S., as seen in the following *Minneapolis Journal* promotion, for which readers predicted the score of the big game. Readers submitted a first guess, a **second guess**, a third guess, and a fourth guess.

Winning Guesses
-----IN THE-----
Journal Want Ad Foot Ball Score Guessing Contest

Each guesser received a ticket, numbered at top, in red, recording each guess.

Winning Guess	Third Guess
6 to 6--Prize $10.00	6 to 11--Prize $5.00
Divided between	Divided between
Nos. 83, 88, 235, 399, 412	Numbers 59, 62, 81, 170, 190, 197, 206, 212, 213, 241, 418, 425 and 440.
Second Guess	**Fourth Guess**
6 to 5---Prize $7.00	6 to 12--Prize $3.00
Divided between	Divided between
Nos. 72, 80, 84, 203, 209, and 414	Nos. 64, 87, 89, 189, 404, 417 and 441.

Parties holding numbered tickets as above will receive their prizes by calling at The Journal office and bringing their tickets.

The Minneapolis Journal contest allowed participants four guesses to predict the final score. ('Winning Guesses, *Minneapolis Journal*, November 2, 1903.)

The first second-guessing in football appeared in 1914 when a reporter countered the critics of the St. John's quarterback after their loss to Maryland.

As a matter of a fact, Heisse used better headwork on first thought than those who accused him of poor headwork after the second guess.[1]

A similar term came to the game via Percy Haughton, who coached Cornell, Harvard, and Columbia. Haughton spent several pages discussing those folks in his 1922 book, *Football, and How to Watch It*. Haughton contended the person in the stands who constantly offered their input was not as well informed as they thought and were not physically and mentally exhausted like the players on the field. While

Haughton did not have a label for these fans, columnists who agreed with his argument in the 1920s called them **grandstand quarterbacks**, a term that was quickly modified.

With fans in the early 1930s listening to radio broadcasts of games at home, often from the comfort of their favorite armchair, they were labeled **armchair quarterbacks**. Similar creatures that consistently questioned players' and coaches' decisions upon returning to work became **Monday morning quarterbacks**.

Art Krenz's cartoon captures the self-righteousness of many Monday morning quarterbacks. (Day, Jim. 'Pipefuls,' *Bakersfield Californian*, October 26, 1936.)

Bowl Game and Bowl Season

Harvard started the college football facilities battle by opening its 42,000-seat football stadium in 1903. Things got crazier in 1914 when Yale opened the 68,000-seat Yale Bowl modeled after Roman amphitheaters. As the first enclosed stadium in the country, it earned the "bowl" description shortly after the design was made public. With fifty percent more seating capacity than the next largest stadium, playing in the Yale Bowl was sometimes described as a "bowl game," and Yale's slate of home games was "bowl season."

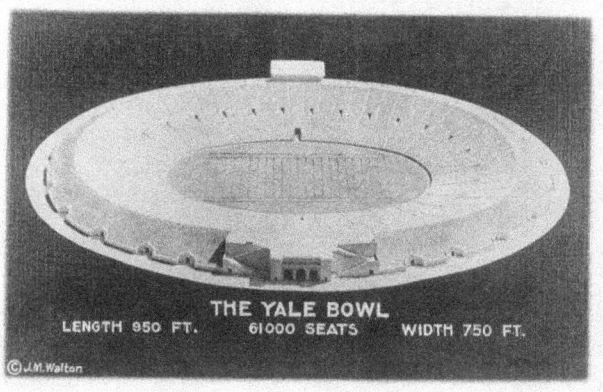

An architect's model of the Yale Bowl from 1913-1914. (Postcard, Personal collection)

Pasadena built its Tournament of Roses Stadium in 1922 to host the annual East-West Football Championship game coinciding with its Tournament of Roses. Despite the stadium being horseshoe-shaped when it opened, a reporter called it the Rose Bowl, and the name stuck.

Rose Bowl Stadium, pictured in 1925, remained a horseshoe until the addition of the southern stands in 1928. (Photographer: Archie M. Dunning, Security Pacific National Bank Collection, Los Angeles Public Library Special Collections)

Many cities hosted post-season games between college or all-star teams in the 1920s, but only the Rose Bowl and the East-West Shrine game survived the early years of the Depression. However, as the nation began recovering, business leaders in some cities used football games to attract tourists. The Orange Bowl debuted in 1934, and the Sugar and Sun Bowls in 1935. **Bowl games** and **bowl season** described the collection of post-season games beginning in 1934 and 1935.

Draft and The Combine

During the NFL's early days, teams could sign any player who would agree to a contract, resulting in franchises with deeper pockets or more competent management signing better players. That changed to some extent in 1936 when the NFL owners opted for an orderly amateur player selection process similar to the military **draft**. However, implementing the draft placed a premium on scouting and assessing eligible talent, an idea lost on the Washington Redskins. They put so few resources into scouting that they drafted UCLA halfback Cal Rossi in the first round of the 1946 draft, not realizing he was a junior and, therefore, not eligible for the draft. They picked him again in the first round of the 1947 draft, despite his intention not to play pro ball, and he never did.

Over time, teams developed scouting departments that visited the big schools while often failing to visit the smaller. The duplication of some efforts and omission of many schools led to the formation of the Lions, Eagles, Steelers Talent Organization (LESTO) in 1964, which allowed the three teams to "combine" their efforts. Other joint scouting services followed.

Further efficiencies came in 1982 when a scouting service invited prospects to a National Invitation Camp to test and evaluate the invited athletes. Rival scouting services developed similar camps before all NFL consolidated their efforts in 1985, giving birth to **The Combine**.

Pass Pattern and Route

Ends and backs went out for passes before the late 1930s but did not run **pass patterns** until then. "Pass" and "pattern" first appeared in combination in the early 1930s as part of a "pass defense pattern," meaning the assignments and alignments defenses used to defend the pass.

"Pass pattern," as used today, entered football's vocabulary due to Dutch Meyer's TCU offense operating under passing tailbacks Sammy Baugh and Davey O'Brien. Meyer modified Pop Warner's Double Wing by splitting the ends wide to stretch the defense and created unique combinations of short and deep routes. He referred to the route combinations as pass patterns, though the term typically refers to individual routes today.

It is worth noting, however, that the previous sentence is misleading because football individual receivers ran "paths" or "courses" in the 1930s and did not run **pass routes** until the 1940s.

———

Flood Pattern. With defenses using six and seven-man lines, there were limited defenders to cover potential pass receivers. That led offenses to send multiple receivers to the right or left and at different depths. By outnumbering the defenders on one side of the ball, the offense flooded the defense, and the tactic became known as the **flood pass** by the end of the 1930s.

7

THE NINETEEN FORTIES

Dropback, Dropback Passer, Dropback Quarterback and Play-Action Pass

The forward pass had numerous restrictions during its first forty years. It started by requiring the passer to be five yards left or right of center when passing. That rule went away in 1910. Instead, passers had to be five yards behind the line of scrimmage when passing until 1946. This requirement and the era's running-oriented offenses contributed to halfbacks or fullbacks being the primary passers. Quarterbacks called the play, took the snap, tossed the ball to a teammate, and then blocked on most plays. They were like fullbacks of recent years, only smart.

The quarterback role changed with the introduction of the Modern T in 1940. The T had the quarterback take the snap from under center, hand off or execute a fake, and then move five or more yards behind the line of scrimmage to throw. The quarterback's last movement became known as dropping back or the **dropback**, though it was not until the early 1950s that the term applied to quarterbacks. (Dropback previously described the location of field goal kickers and punters behind the line of scrimmage.) In addition, **dropback passer** did not arrive until 1958, while **dropback quarterback** first appeared in 1964.

The delay in acquiring a name for the technique may have been due to the inconsistency in quarterback actions. College and NFL films of the 1940s and 1950s show quarterbacks seldom using the regimented dropback technique that became common in the 1960s. Instead, they meandered back, backpedaled, and scrambled when the pass protection was poor. However, revised blocking rules and the development of pocket or cup pass protection soon changed that situation.

Other methods of slowing the pass rush included screen passes, bootlegs, and the fakes incorporated into the ball handling of dropback quarterbacks. While Sonny Jurgensen and the Eagles were the first to be mentioned in print, Hank Stram raised these fakes to a high level when coaching the Kansas City Chiefs. They threw the ball after showing running play action, leading to **play-action pass** entering the game's vocabulary in the 1960s.

Handoff and Modern T Formation

One might think the term **handoff** was always part of football, yet it took seventy years to arrive on the scene. While some passes from the quarterback fit our definition of a handoff from a technique standpoint, they did not use the term, though some referred to it as a direct pass. For example, the images and descriptions below from Pop Warner's *Football for Players and Coaches* (published in 1912) show the quarterback handing the ball to the running back on the plunge or dive play (image on left). Yet Warner refers to the "handoff" and the toss for the sweep (image on right) as passes.

The first snap-shot shows a pass for a line plunge, and the other for a play outside of tackle. Note that in the line plunge the quarter has placed the ball against the runner's stomach, and is holding it there while the latter is closing his hands and arms upon it.

(Warner, 1912)

Before 1941, "handoff" seldom appeared in football literature and, when used, typically reflected its rugby meaning, where handoff was synonymous with a stiff or straight arm.

The arrival of the new handoff in the early 1940s stems from a rule change and the emergence of two new offenses. The rule change came in 1941 when backs were first allowed to hand the ball forward to teammates, provided the exchange was hand-to-hand and occurred behind the line of scrimmage. Allowing forward handoffs heightened the distinction between handing and passing the ball to a teammate.

The second influence was the emergence of the **Modern T** and Split T offenses. Both placed the quarterback under center, who, after taking the snap, often gave or faked a handoff on a halfback dive. The Split T quarterback followed the dive fake with football's first option wide, further emphasizing the distinction between handoffs and passes or tosses.

To distinguish Halas and Shaughnessy's T formation from its predecessors, it was called the Modern T starting in 1940 but typically was referred to simply as the T formation.

Modern T

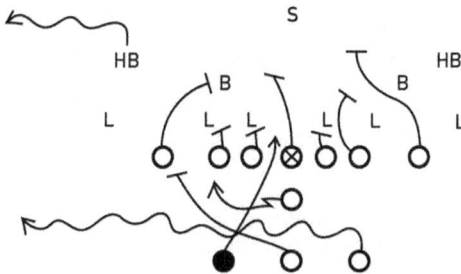

The Modern T quarterback sometimes handed off the ball along the line, dropped back, or rolled out.

Single-Platoon and Two-Platoon

America began mobilizing for war before Pearl Harbor, leading coaches to voice concerns about lean rosters. The 1941 rules committee approved unlimited substitutions to address those fears, allowing players to leave and reenter the game whenever the ball was dead. Intended as a temporary rule, the rules committee and everyone else expected to insert one or two substitutes as short-term relief. That is how coaches applied the rule until Michigan's Fritz Crisler gambled on a new approach against a superior opponent in 1945.

Leading up to Michigan's game with a dominant West Point team, Crisler created separate offensive and defensive units and swapped them with each change of possession. Swapping offensive and defensive units became known as **two-platoon** football, and playing both ways became **single-platoon** football.

Interestingly, Red Blaik, Army's coach, is widely credited with coining those terms, but that does not appear to be the case. While "platoon" was long a military term, "two-platoon" had referred to rotating 12-hour shifts in American police and fire departments since the 1870s. Moreover, "two-platoon" was used in football to describe the shock troop units used by Frank Leahy's 1940 Boston College and Buff Donelli's 1942 Duquesne teams. So, platooning was part of football before the 1941 substitution rule came into effect.

Clothesline Tackle

In the days before households had gas or electric dryers, people hung their wet garb on ropes or clotheslines. The tautness of those ropes must have impressed a few folks since clothesline became a positive attribute in several sports. For example, clothesline hits in baseball, golf shots, and football passes were akin to line drives or throwing ropes.

That changed in the early 1940s when a football tackle made by extending the arm and striking the ball carrier in the neck or head became known as a **clothesline tackle**.

Two-Minute Warning, Run Out the Clock, Two-Minute Drill, and Spike the Ball

When football began, teams played two forty-five-minute innings or halves. The halves were reduced to thirty-five minutes in 1894, to thirty-minute halves in 1906, and then shifted to four fifteen-minute quarters in 1910. The referee and later other officials kept track of the time using a pocket watch or stopwatch. Scoreboard clocks did not exist, so one of the officiating crew alerted the team captains of the time remaining on the clock. Football's 1888 rule book stated, "The referee shall notify the captains of the time remaining not more than ten nor less than five minutes from the end of each half."[1] Later, the responsibility shifted to the linesman and then the field judge, who provided the remaining time to the team captains upon request.

In 1926, Wisconsin installed the first scoreboard clock for which time-keepers on the sideline monitored the officials' whistles in an attempt to display the approximate time remaining in the quarter. By the mid-1930s, the scoreboard clock became the official time source at many major college stadiums.

As scoreboard clocks became increasingly available, teams could better monitor the time and adjust their play calling based on the game situation. Although teams had managed the clock in the past, the early 1940s saw the first references to teams **running out the clock** by calling running plays to keep the game clock ticking.

The NFL took a different path when they adopted a rule in 1949 to notify teams and stop the clock with two minutes left on the clock, a step now known as the **two-minute warning**. However, the NFL retained the two-minute warning when the stadium clock became the official timepiece, likely because the stoppage allowed another commercial break.

The two-minute warning is most meaningful in close games, as when Vince Lombardi's Green Bay Packers lost to the Philadelphia Eagles as time ran out in the 1960 NFL Championship game. The story goes that following that loss, Lombardi instituted weekly practice drills to simulate having less than two minutes on the clock. As a result, that portion of practice became known as the **two-minute drill**. Unfortunately for that story, Iowa State and, perhaps others, ran two-minute drills during their 1960 season training camp, so Vince likely did not start those drills. Either way, the term transferred over from the drills to describe teams running their quick offense in late-game situations.

The emphasis on two-minute drills led to several rule changes that allowed teams to manage the clock more effectively. Starting in 1982, the NCAA allowed quarterbacks to throw the ball out of bounds to stop the clock. Since throwing the ball out of bounds allowed several seconds to tick off the clock, the 1989 NFL and 1990 NCAA rules allowed quarterbacks to **spike** the ball to stop the clock.

Delay of Game

For years, football officials had the discretion to penalize teams they believed to be stalling. That allowed officials who did not care for huddling when it started in the early 1920s to step off penalties on huddling teams. Sentiments quickly shifted, and the officials stopped penalizing teams if they snapped the ball within a reasonable time (thirty seconds or so).

Concerns about stalling rose again in 1941 due to the rule allowing unlimited substitutions when the clock stopped, which happened following a score, during a point after attempt, after a fair catch or incomplete pass, when the ball went out of bounds, and while enforcing or declining a penalty. Teams wanting to substitute a player while the clock was running had to call a timeout.

Due to concerns that teams might take too much time selecting and sending in substitutes - a **delay of game**- football added a rule requiring the ball to be snapped within 25 seconds of the referee spotting the ball.

Taxi Squad, Injured Reserve List, and Physically Unable to Perform (PUP) List

Among the challenges facing teams needing to meet roster limits is handling developmental and injured players. Early leagues did not always have effective methods to address these issues, so teams found ways to circumvent the existing rules.

The Cleveland Brown were charter members of the All-American Football Conference in 1946 and sought to discourage certain players they cut from signing with other teams. Select players cut by the Browns continued practicing with the team but were unpaid while waiting for a roster spot. Instead, they earned money working for a taxi company owned by the Browns' owner, Arthur McBride. Known as the **taxi squad**, a similar and formal mechanism for non-roster players became a part of the NFL roster management processes after the Browns joined the NFL.

A similar issue at the time involved allowing injured players to remain under contract while not counting against the roster limit. The first mention of a player placed on the **injured reserve list** came in 1947 when the Bethlehem Bulldogs of the post-WWII American Football League placed Ray Stengel on injured reserve. The next mention of the injured reserve list involved the AAFC's Cleveland Browns. Then, in 1949, the NFL announced it was amending the injured reserve list to keep teams from hiding players. Previously, players could move from the injured reserve list to active status, but the 1949 rule required players on the list to sit for the entire year unless they cleared waivers.

Another iteration of these mechanisms is the **physically unable to perform list**, which arose in 1970. Its shorthand name, PUP list, arrived ten years later. The PUP list has variously dealt with players returning from football injuries, those unable to play due to non-football issues, and the like.

Blitz and Red Dog

Blitzkrieg (German for lighting war) entered America's foreign affairs and military conversations in 1938 to describe the potential of Germany's quick-strike tactics. Within two weeks of Germany's using blitzkrieg tactics during its September 1939 invasion of Poland, **blitz** and blitzkrieg entered the vocabulary of America's football writers. However, nearly every use of those terms for the next twenty years described teams with quick-strike offenses or those that overwhelmed an opponent. Blitz did not become a term to describe a defensive tactic until the late 1950s.

The tactic we now refer to as blitzing was initially called a **red dog** or **red dogging**, often said to originate with Don "Red" Ettinger, an All-Pro rookie for the New York Giants in 1948. Athletic enough to play guard on Kansas' basketball team, Ettinger rushed the quarterback shortly after the snap while the tackles dogged or stunted outside. Ettinger's nickname and the tackles "dogging" led to the tactic being called the red dog or red dogging. "Red dog" fell out of use in the early 1960s, with blitz becoming the preferred term for the tactic.

Penalty Flag, Laundry on the Field, and Yellow Laundry

Play stopped in early football only when the tackled player yelled, "Down." That changed in 1887 when football began using the newly invented Acme pea whistle to signal the end of the play. Unfortunately, officials also blew their whistles when fouls occurred -often in the middle of a play- so players and everyone else became confused, sometimes stopping play when the ball remained live.

A 1904 rule change took the whistle out of officials' hands and mouths other than the referee's. The other officials used bells or horns to signal penalties. Bells never caught on, but horns did, including kazoo-like devices often worn on a wristband. Despite the difference in sound, some players remained confused by the horn-blowing.

While umpires and linesmen were tooting their horns to signal penalties, a few officials in the 1930s reportedly dropped handkerchiefs to indicate where fouls occurred. However, football's conversion to throwing flags for penalties is due to Dwight "Dike" Beede, Youngstown State's coach.

Beede asked his wife to sew a handful of small, weighted flags for officials to throw instead of blowing their horns. The Betsy Ross of football created a set of striped penalty flags using spare fabric. Beede then convinced the opposing coach and the officiating crew to use the flags in Youngstown State's game with Oklahoma City University in 1941.

One of Irma Beede's original penalty flags. (Courtesy of Chick-fil-A College Football Hall of Fame)

People continued referring to the flags as handkerchiefs until 1945, when **penalty flag** first appeared in the coverage of high school games. The NCAA officially adopted penalty flags in 1948. However, the rules instructed the officials other than the referee to continue using horns or bells while also dropping a "marker" when spotting a foul.

Early penalty flags were generally white, shifted to red, and then orange due to the latter being more visible on color televisions. In 1953, the NFL rules committee considered having officials throw flags of one color for offensive penalties and another for defensive penalties, but they opted not to adopt the rule.

The mid-1970s saw thrown penalty flags begin to be referred to as **laundry on the field** or **yellow laundry**. Still, the expression appears to have been used more often by radio and television announcers than by those in the print press.

Option Play and Split T

Among the most significant innovations in offensive football has been **option play**. The first plays described as options involved tailbacks or halfbacks rolling out with the choice to run or pass. The plays we now consider run options (as opposed to run-pass options or RPOs) arrived when Don Faurot introduced the Split T offense at Missouri in 1941. Though referred to simply as a "T Offense," people began calling it the **Split T** in 1944 to distinguish it from the Modern T of Chicago Bears and Stanford fame.

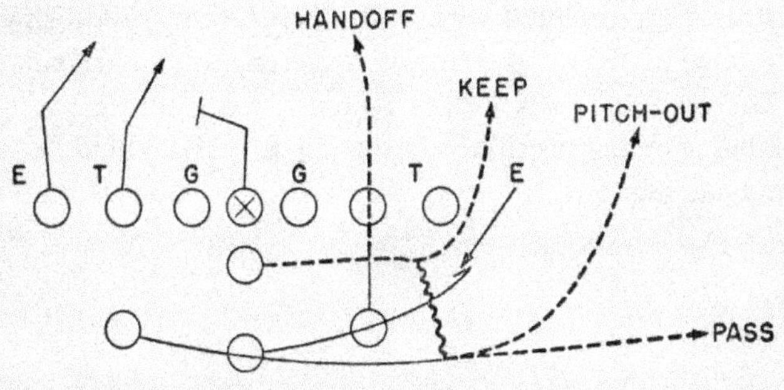

Fig. 5. Sequence of basic plays.

The Split T predetermined the fake or handoff to the playside halfback. They called one or the other in the huddle, so it was not an option. Only the keep versus pitch and the halfback's run-pass decisions were options. (Faurot, 1950)

It is worth noting that Faurot did not refer to the play as an option; he called the sequence the keep and running pitchout. By 1949, however, others referred to the Split T sequence as an option play, and the term became dominant. (In his 1950 book, *Football: The Secrets of the "Split-T" Formation*, Faurot said, "The quarterback has the option of pitching the ball for the play around the end, or of keeping the ball and continuing inside."[2])

The Split T was college football's dominant option offense in the 1950s, with Oklahoma and Maryland riding it to national championships. Of course, other option offenses emerged in the 1960s.

Back or Sideline Judge

The NFL stopped using the college rule book in 1933, leading to rule differences between the college and pro games that leaked over to the officiating crews and responsibilities in 1947 when the NFL added the **back** or **sideline judge**. Positioned a few yards behind the line of scrimmage along the sideline opposite the head linesman, the back judge focused on illegal motion and shifts in the offensive backfield, allowing the referee to focus on the quarterback (and unofficially protect the drop-back quarterbacks emerging as stars in the passing-oriented pro game). The back judge also monitored his sideline, adding another set of eyes on plays downfield.

The Big Ten experimented with a fifth official in 1950, formally adding the back judge in 1951. Other major conferences followed suit during the 1950s. The field and back judges switched roles during the 1950s, with the back judge being positioned in the defensive backfield to monitor the downfield passing.

The SEC had a back judge in 1954 when Kentucky threw a flood pass with receivers at three levels. (1956 *Kentuckian*, University of Kentucky Special Collections and Research Center.)

Pocket and Cup Pass Protection

The Single Wing and Notre Dame Box offenses relied on misdirection, rollouts, and bootlegs to supplement the pass protection provided by the linemen. Still, passers often had limited time to find an open receiver and toss the ball. Much of the challenge stemmed from the blocking rules of the 1930s and 1940s, which prohibited blockers from extending their arms. Limitations in pass protection also came from the failure to think of pass blocking as fundamentally different than run blocking.

Linemen of the era used drive blocking or rolling / body blocks to shield defenders. While one or two offensive linemen might successfully drive block their opponent using these techniques, they risked opening gaps for defenders to run through. Likewise, body blocking tended to delay rather than stop a rusher, giving the quarterback some time but not enough.

The Modern T and its dropback quarterback increased the focus on pass protection. Successful offensive lines sometimes received praise for providing "pockets of protection," though it is unclear that the protection stemmed from new tactics and concepts. However, by the middle of the 1940s, strategies began to change, with linemen -especially tackles- taught to drop step with the outside leg and give ground, forming a protective cup around the quarterback.

As Dana X. Bible's noted in his *Championship Football*:

> The center and guards may remain in place, or they may hit any opponents in front of them with a quick jab step and shield block and immediately retreat to their original position. The tackles drop back about two yards, and two backs are assigned to the zones just outside the tackles.[3]

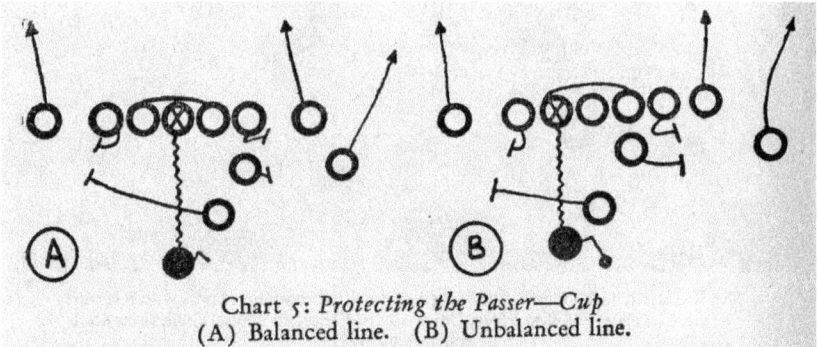

Chart 5: *Protecting the Passer—Cup*
(A) Balanced line.   (B) Unbalanced line.

Bible's illustration of cup protection in unbalanced or balanced formations. (Bible, 1947)

Cup protection and **pocket protection** entered football's mainstream language in the late 1940s. Paul Brown's Cleveland Browns used the principles to protect Otto Graham en route to four consecutive AAFC championships from 1946 to 1949. Bob Neyland also received credit for introducing cup protection to the South, but the evidence of him doing so before Dana X. Bible is thin.

Draw Play

The story goes that in an early 1940s game between the Chicago Bears and Green Bay Packers, Packers linebacker Buckets Goldenberg spotted a tell or difference in Sid Luckman's stance on plays he dropped back to pass in the Bears T formation. Goldenberg quickly dropped into pass coverage when he saw the tell, and the Bears center, Bulldog Turner, picked up Goldenberg's tendency. He suggested the Bears fake the dropback and give the ball to fullback Bill Osmanski on a delayed handoff. The play proved successful and is said to be the origin of the **draw play**.

A challenge concerning that story is that "draw play" does not appear in print until North Carolina's Carl Snavely commented on Rice's effective use of draw plays in the 1950 Cotton Bowl, suggesting the draw play went by an alternative name until the late 1940s.

Granddaddy of Them All

There is no joy in taking down a legend, but the truth must prevail in the search for the origins of football terminology. So here's the truth: Keith Jackson neither coined the phrase, **The Granddaddy of Them All,** nor was he the first to associate it with the Rose Bowl, and it's not even close.

The Granddaddy of Them All originally and still means the first, oldest, or best of something. It first appeared in print to describe an unusually large raccoon caught in Nebraska in 1897. Over the next several decades, it applied to all manner of things. Its first link to football came in 1932 when USC's quarterback, Orv Mohler, was called the Granddaddy of Them All because he was older than his teammates at 23 years old. The 1930s also saw the phrase used to describe the Notre Dame-USC and the Harvard-Yale series. During the same decades, its first connection to the Rose Bowl came when sportswriters deemed Columbia's upset victory over Stanford in the 1934 Rose Bowl the sports story of the year and, therefore, the Granddaddy of Them All.

A key moment, however, came on January 1, 1949, as the 35th Rose Bowl loomed. The headline of a Louisiana newspaper's preview of Northwestern's first appearance in the Rose Bowl read:

Northwestern Favored for 'Granddaddy of Them All'[4]

From then on, Granddaddy of Them All was a common description for the Rose Bowl, particularly after 1970. The phrase became so closely tied to the Rose Bowl that the Tournament of Roses printed the slogan on the Rose Bowl game tickets from 1977 to 1987 and from 2016 to 2019.

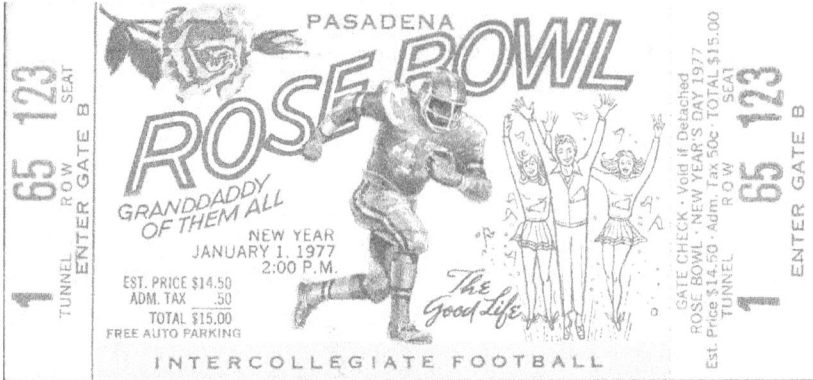

The 1977 game tickets included the Granddaddy slogan for the first time.

Critically, while Keith Jackson handled the television play-by-play for fifteen Rose Bowls, his first came in 1989, after the slogan had appeared on game tickets for eleven straight years. In the end, Keith Jackson had a wonderful connection to the Rose Bowl and to the Granddaddy phrase, but the idea that Keith Jackson coined or popularized the phrase is untrue.

8

THE NINETEEN FIFTIES

Playbook

While coaches began authoring books in the 1890s that included play diagrams and individual player assignments, players learned those plays on the field, in chalk talks, or by studying notes they took during the chalk talks. Coaches do not appear to have issued playbooks until the early 1950s, likely due to costs and other printing or copying limitations.

Reporters in the 1940s mention playbooks but use the term metaphorically. In the early 1950s, however, stories emerged of coaches preparing and distributing **playbooks** to their players, though some items distributed might be considered scouting reports today.

Paul Brown often receives credit for being the first coach to test his players on their knowledge of the playbook contents. Still, Paul Brown's 1954 Cleveland Browns playbook has handwritten notes and player movements drawn on preprinted forms, so it is unclear when Brown first distributed completed playbooks to his teams. At least one other NFL team is known to have used pre-printed or mimeographed playbooks that year.

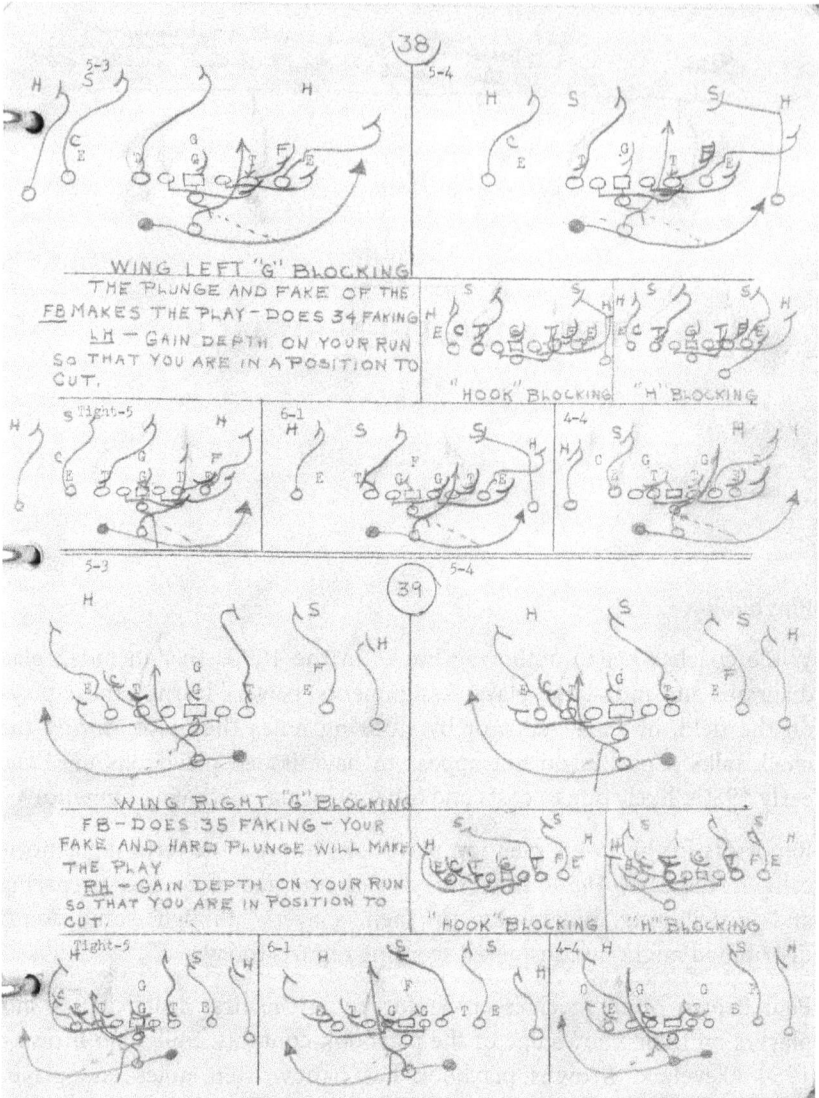

Page showing the 38 and 38 Sweep from the 1954 Cleveland Browns playbook. (Image courtesy of the Walter Havighurst Special Collections, Miami University Libraries. Oxford, Ohio.)

Stunt, Audible, Reading Defenses, and Hut

The post-WWII rise of professional and two-platoon football brought greater specialization, allowing more complexity, including offenses using multiple formations, motions, protections, routes, and more. Possessing substantially more plays and adjustments than in the past, teams could no longer name their plays by numbers because players could not memorize all the plays by rote.

The 1954 Washington Redskins had more than 450 plays and combinations, so they replaced play numbering with strings of information that included assignments. An example play call in the huddle was: "Left 2, 37 F U Z O, on 3."[1] Left 2 identified the formation with the left halfback flanking left, 37 told the fullback to run the ball through the seven hole, F U Z O provided blocking assignments, and 3 was the snap count. (College football returned to single-platoon football in 1952, so most major college offenses remained simple enough to continue naming plays using numbers only.)

With offenses no longer aligning in the same formation play after play, defenses became less predictable, switching formations and assignments situationally. Post-snap movements by defensive linemen slanting in one direction or another, linebacker blitzes, and other tricks became known as **stunts**.

The result was that the play called in the offensive huddle did not always match well with the defense they faced. That led offenses to switch plays at the line of scrimmage via the quarterback's **audible** signals. (Audibles were called "automatics" by some teams.)

The quarterback's ability to recognize the defensive alignment and their actions once the play began became critical to quarterbacks distributing the call properly on many running and pass plays. Thus, quarterbacks of the 1950s needed the ability to **read defenses**.

Quarterback cadences also changed in the post-WWII era when offenses borrowed from the military yet again. The military's "Atten-hut" and "hut, hut" while marching entered football cadences with "Set, ready, hike, **hut** one, hut two, hut three" becoming a common sequence.

Swing Pass or Route

The meaning of some terms evolve, others have multiple definitions, while others have unclear meanings. Such is the case with **swing pass** or **swing route**. Swing pass shows up in early 1940s game reports, but its meaning is unclear, mainly because some used "swing pass" and bootleg pass interchangeably in the 1940s.

By the early 1950s, however, play diagrams included in articles confirm that "swing pass" had taken on its current meaning: a route typically run by a running back, who runs toward the sideline and behind the line of scrimmage while looking for the ball over his inside shoulder.

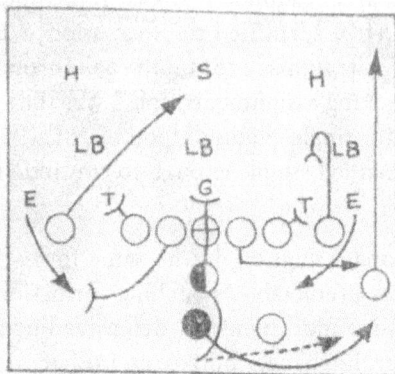

The diagram shows LSU's fullback executing a swing pass out of their pro formation. (Fleming, Ed, 'LSU Offense Is Mainly Strong Pass Formation,' *Austin American-Statesman*, September 16, 1954.)

Ball Control Offense

Ball-control offense arrived in 1934 to describe USC's basketball team, then coached by Sam Berry. Besides creating basketball's triangle offense and leading efforts to eliminate the center jump after each made shot, Berry was USC's head baseball coach and functioned as what is now considered the defensive coordinator for USC's football team.

"Ball-control offense" remained a California-only term in the 1930s before dribbling onto the nation's basketball courts in the 1940s. Its first use in football concerned Texas' offense in their victory over Tennessee in the 1953 Cotton Bowl. Under second-year coach Ed Price, Texas ran the Split-T. Ball control was an apt description for the Longhorn's Cotton Bowl performance since they gained 269 yards rushing and 32 passing. Tennessee, in Bob Neyland's last game as coach, lost 14 yards rushing and gained 46 yards passing.

Jones hands off to Quinn who scored second Texas touchdown

Longhorn quarterback T. Jones hands off to Billy Quinn on a goal-line dive play for the second touchdown of Texas' 16-0 win in the 1953 Cotton Bowl. (*The Volunteer*, 1953. Yearbook of the University of Tennessee, Knoxville, University of Tennessee, Knoxville – Libraries)

From that point, the term applied to run-heavy offenses until the emergence of the high-percentage West Coast passing offense in the mid-1980s.

Nose Bumper

The introduction of plastic football helmets in 1940 offered dramatically increased protection for the wearer at the expense of potential injuries to others on the field. Unfortunately, early plastic helmets were shaped much like their leather predecessors, introducing two new injury sources. Since players secured the early plastic helmets with two-point chin straps, the helmets were subject to being pushed back against the neck and forward against the nose, leading to broken necks and noses.

To address these issues in the mid-1950s, helmet manufacturers trimmed the helmet edges with leather-covered pads and raised the back of helmets to eliminate the guillotine effect of earlier models. Borrowing from the automotive industry, the edging and padding on the helmet's front became known as a **nose bumper**.

The white trim along the edge of the helmet became known as the most bumper.
(Wilson Fall Winter Catalog, 1956-57 Trade Price Edition)

Helmet technology and designs changed, and the 1970s introduction of the four-point chin strap reduced the helmet's back-and-forth movement. Nose bumpers remained, however, and became more prominent, especially the portion immediately above the bridge of the nose. In addition, the advent of equipment brand logos on athletic gear led to nose bumpers becoming the location for helmet manufacturers' logos. Of course, nose bumpers often display conference or team logos today.

Introduced in the late 1980a, the Riddell VSR1 featured a
prominent nose bumper with the Riddell logo. (Riddell VSR1
Helmet Care and Fitting Instructions)

Three Yards and A Cloud of Dust

Few expressions are more closely associated with a particular football coach than the link between "three yards and a cloud of dust" and Woody Hayes. Yet, while the two are tied together in people's minds today, they were not linked originally.

Old-time football fields were not watered and often became dusty, particularly out West, where the lack of rain left football fields with little grass. Other parts of the country also experienced periodic dry spells and played games in baseball parks where dust kicked up on the infield. So, dust clouds were a regular part of football in the old days and remain in a few locales today.

Dust kicks up from the infield at Braves Park during the 1952 Holy Cross-Boston College game. (1953 *Holy Cross Purple Patcher,* College of the Holy Cross Archives)

Three yards and a cloud of dust is an expression of pride for those who enjoy marching down the field methodically. However, others consider it a pejorative for a dated, dull, and unimaginative style of play. The latter was its original meaning when used to describe Split T offenses in the 1950s. Although teams found success using the Split T, college football's run-heavy, limited substitution game of the 1950s contrasted with the increasingly popular NFL with star quarterbacks and pass-heavy game.

Split T

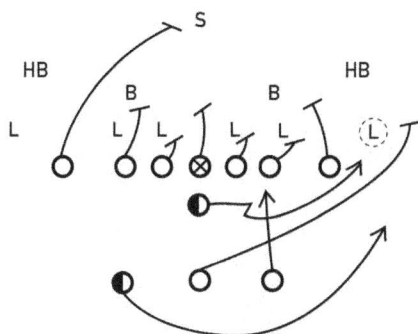

Faurot's Split T added horizontal space between the offensive linemen, faked to the dive back, and optioned the last defender on the line of scrimmage.

The Split T was the brainchild of Don Faurot, who introduced it at Missouri in 1941 as football's first option running attack. As in the Modern T, the quarterback placed his hands under center. His first post-snap movement was to give to or fake the quick-hitting halfback dive. (The quarterback called the give or fake in the huddle; it was not an option read.) After the give or fake, the quarterback moved along the line of scrimmage and read the unblocked defensive end. If the defensive end penetrated the backfield or moved outside, the quarterback kept the ball, turning upfield. Conversely, if the defensive end attacked the quarterback, the quarterback pitched to the sweeping halfback using an underhand toss.

Since the quarterback ran directly behind the line of scrimmage on the base series, he was not five yards behind the line of scrimmage and could not legally throw a forward pass until the college rules changed in 1945. Even after the rule change, Split T quarterbacks remained too close to the line to pass effectively, so the halfbacks handled the passing, as they did in the Single Wing.

A few coaches, including Cactus Jack Curtice, passed the ball extensively in the 1950s. Curtice coached in Texas before taking over at Utah in 1950, where he won the Skyline Conference in 1951, 1952, and 1953 with a pass-happy offense. For the next several years, however, he ran the ball more using elements of the Split T, which John Mooney, a writer for the Salt Lake Tribune, found boring, as he told his readers on several occasions.

A Mooney article leading up to the 1955 Utah-BYU game mentioned that Max Tolbert, a BYU assistant, referred to the Split T as "a cloud of dust and four yards." While Tolbert is the first person known to have combined yardage and a dust cloud, but it is unclear whether he coined the phrase or was simply the first to be quoted using it.

BYU's 1956 coaching staff. Max Tolbert is second from right. (Courtesy, L. Tom Perry Special Collections, Harold B. Lee Library, Brigham Young University)

Mooney later changed the line to "a cloud of dust and five yards" in articles in 1956 and 1957 before returning to the four yards version later in 1957. The expression also popped up toward the end of the 1957 season when Louisiana sports columnist, Jim Wynn, commented on Texas A&M's poor showing versus Texas, saying:

> The Aggies showed little or no offensive imagination in the game with Texas. Texas A&M's passing attack was weak, almost to the point of non-existence. The big Aggies play was a quick **three-yards-and-a-cloud-of-dust** burst into the middle of the line.[2]

That article marked the first time "three yards and a cloud of dust" appeared in print. It is worth noting that the unimaginative Texas A&M coach he disparaged was a fellow named Bear Bryant, who, within the week, resigned from Texas A&M to return home to Alabama.

During the 1958 season, writers generally used "three yards and a cloud of dust" when referring to Split T, Southwest Conference teams, and South Carolina and Ohio State. Similar comments appeared about cloud dusters other than Ohio State during the 1959 season. Still, the expression became inextricably linked to Ohio State after Woody Hayes embraced the phrase while speaking at a 1959 coaching clinic:

> ... some newspapermen call our attack 'three yards and a cloud of dust.' But we don't care what the offense is called as long as it wins football games. I'm willing to take three and one-third yards on every play and force the other guy to make mistakes.[3]

Woody's embrace of power football and contempt for sportswriters resulted in his version of Ohio State football being forever tied to dust clouds.

Slotback, X, Y, and Z, Tight End, and Wideout

The rise of the Modern T formation reshaped football as teams began positioning an end wide to spread the defense and facilitate that player's release into passing routes. Likewise, they motioned a halfback into a flanking position before deciding to skip the motion and position the flanker wide directly from the huddle.

Stanford's Gallarneau (#29), in motion on the 50-yard line, draws the Nebraska
defensive halfback to the outside during the 1941 Rose Bowl. (Unpublished
snapshot, Personal collection)

In the 1956 season, several NFL teams placed a halfback between the split end and offensive tackle to create the **slotback**. The following year, the Detroit Lion distinguished the end that split wide from the end that remained tight to the formation, naming the latter the **tight end**. The distinction caught on; by 1959, numerous NFL and college teams made the same distinction. Over time, the split and tight end roles became specialized, and their physical requirements diverged. Tight ends continued in-line blocking, so they retained some characteristics of offensive linemen. In contrast, split ends were valued for their speed, route running, and catching ability, so their size became relatively less important.

Sid Gillman introduced another innovation in terminology in the 1950s when he brought his run-oriented Spin T offense from Miami (OH) to the Los Angeles Rams in 1955. Having access to a highly-skilled quarterback like Norm Van Brocklin, Gillman switched to a sophisticated passing offense. To simplify the playbook, play calling, and other communication, Gillman called the wide receiver the **X**, the tight end the **Y**, and the flanker the **Z**.

Then, in 1966, college teams in the Southeast, such as Florida with quarterback Steve Spurrier, ran formations splitting both ends. To distinguish one from the other, they called one the split end and the other the **wideout**. That distinction quickly disappeared, and wideout soon meant any eligible receiver aligning wide.

Middle Guard, Nose Guard, Nose Tackle, Gap Responsibility, and Two-Gap Responsibility

The expanding passing game post-WWII required defenses to find ways to limit the passing attacks. A primary solution was to shift personnel from the line to linebacking or secondary defensive roles. That meant switching from 6-man to 5-man lines, often moving from a 6-2 to a 5-3 defense.

These defensive changes and the growth of two-platoon football created the need to name certain defensive positions instead of referring to them by players' offensive positions. For example, among defensive linemen, the player aligned over the center in a 5-man defense became the **middle guard**.

In the late 1950s, Bud Wilkinson devised the 5-2 Oklahoma defense to deal with Split-T offenses. Rather than refer to the player over the center as the middle guard, they called him a **nose guard**. Then, in the late 1960s, *nose-guard tackle* entered the game, later morphing to **nose tackle**.

Finally, while defensive players had long been responsible for specific spaces or gaps between offensive linemen, it was not until 1968 that Al Herring, the Atlanta Falcons' defensive coordinator, told his linemen they had **gap responsibility**. Likewise, despite the idea of "two-gap responsibility" originating in the 1950s with the Oklahoma 5-2, **two-gap responsibility** did not enter football's vocabulary until 1976.

Middle Linebacker, Outside Linebacker, and Cornerback

The passing game advances that changed the defensive line alignments and responsibilities also forced changes at the linebacker and secondary levels. While there had been 6-3 defenses in the 1930s, the 6-3 and 5-3 defenses of the 1940s were designed to combat the modern T formation's dives, man-in-motion, and passing attack. The focus on the passing attack led to distinguishing each linebacker's responsibilities and assigning new names: **middle linebacker** versus **outside linebackers**. Middle linebackers were also called *center linebackers*, and outside linebackers were often called *corner linebacker*s until the mid-1960s.

Yet another position emerged in the mid-1950s as NFL teams shifted to the 4-3 defense. Two safeties were positioned deep and in the middle of the field, while two other defensive halfbacks played shallow and wide. Being placed in the corners of the defense, they became **cornerbacks**.

Mike, Sam, and Will Linebacker, Free Safety and Strong Safety

The New York Giants' defensive staff in the 1950s included Tom Landry as a player-coach and, later, defensive coordinator. In 1956, Landry modified the Giants' 5-2 defense by eliminating the defensive lineman aligned over the center and replacing him with the middle linebacker, so the three linebackers and four down linemen formed the 4-3 defense. However, Landry made a mistake with his version of the 4-3 by calling the three linebacking positions Sarah (strong side), Meg (middle), and Wanda (weak side), a naming convention quickly rejected by others.

The following year the Los Angeles Rams called their middle linebacker **Mike**. **Sam** and **Will** soon followed. (Mike had previously been the name for the Rams' middle guard.)

Initially, the two safeties in the 4-3 defense had comparable roles and were called the right and left safeties. However, when offenses specialized their ends, one splitting out and the other remaining tight, defenses mirrored that distinction and distinguished the safety roles. The safety on the tight or strong side became the **strong safety** by 1958. At the same time, the cornerbacks and strong safety often played man-to-man coverage, allowing the other safety to roam free, so he became the **free safety**.

Prevent Defense

The early forward pass came with many restrictions due to an underlying belief that completing passes involved substantial luck. Specifically, in the low-scoring games of the time, traditionalists did not want teams getting lucky and winning a game via a long touchdown pass.

As restrictions on the passing game eased in the 1930s and 1940s, offenses flung the ball around more often, became more adept at it, and defenses adjusted accordingly. One element of those adjustments came in the mid-1950s as teams softened their coverage late in close games to stop those lucky, long passes. Since these defenses allowed the completion of short passes while preventing long passes, the approach became known as the **prevent defense**.

Offensive and Defensive Coordinator

The player specialization resulting from two-platoon football had a reciprocal relationship with the coaching staff. In the single-platoon days, coaches had less time to develop new approaches, create game plans for both sides of the ball, and impart that information to those playing both ways. As a result, football techniques and strategies were less complicated.

However, two-platoon football separated teams into offensive and defensive squads, and coaching staffs expanded to prepare the separate units in practice. Larger staffs led to head coaches delegating authority to assistants called the *head offensive coach* or *head defensive coach* in the early 1950s. That remained the accepted nomenclature through the 1950s except at Iowa, where Forest Evashevski named Jerry Burns his **Defensive Coordinator**. Defensive and **Offensive Coordinator** roles appeared at Cornell and Ohio State in 1961, and from that point on, coordinator became the standard description for those roles.

Hearing Footsteps and Alligator Arms

Since receivers first went downfield and stretched out for passes, they have sensed defensive players' willingness to introduce themselves with a violent hit. Part of anticipating the coming collision involved listening for the sound of the defenders' approach, causing some receivers to drop the ball. The name for this situation first appeared in print in 1955 when Ottawa Rough Riders assistant coach Tom McHugh noted that the "...Montreal receivers have been **hearing footsteps** all night."[4]

Later that season, Tom Fears, then a split end with the Los Angeles Rams, was asked whether there was a secret to his ability to catch everything thrown his way. Fears responded:

You just have to blank yourself out to everything else. You can't be thinking which way you're going after the ball arrives, how many yards you need and particularly whether some monster is about to clobber you. We call that last little item 'hearing footsteps.'[5]

A similar expression appeared in print in 1987 when New York Giants' players commented on their victory over the Washington Redskins in the NFC championship game. The Giants said they noticed Redskins receivers with **alligator arms** after being consistently hit by the Giants defenders.

Kevin Steele, then the defensive backs coach at Tennessee, indicated months later that he coined the expression while coaching at Oklahoma State from 1984 to 1987. Per Steele, the Tennessee defensive backs' goal was to "hit a receiver so hard and so often they'll catch the ball like an alligator,"[6] so Greene appears to be the expression's originator.

Gunner

Most words entering the football vocabulary gain widespread use soon after their introduction. Words either make it or they don't, and the process happens quickly. However, some terms gestate for a time before gaining traction. One of those was the name for players responsible for covering punts and tackling the returner.

Two ends release from their split positions in punt formation. The defense does not impede either end near the line of scrimmage. (Zuppke, 1924)

The Marshalltown High School (Iowa) coaches referred to a speedy end who covered punts as the **gunner** in 1956. Perhaps it was a passing comment or one-time use because the term did not reappear in discussions of punt coverage discussions until it arrived in Green Bay in 1977.

The appearance of "gunner" in 1977 likely stems from a 1974 NFL rule to encourage more punt returns by prohibiting all but two members of the punting team from crossing the line of scrimmage before the punter kicked the ball. The logic of the rule was that eligible receivers on the line of scrimmage had to be allowed to go downfield immediately since they might catch a pass on a fake punt. One or two other teams referred to these players as gunners at the time, but the term fizzled again.

Finally, gunner reappeared in Green Bay in 1988 when rookie safety Chuck Cecil made his mark in the NFL through his aggressive special teams play. The term's usage increased over the next several seasons and entered the mainstream by the mid-1990s.

North-South Runner

By tradition and not by rule, one end zone sits at the north end of the field, the other at the south end, and the home team bench typically sits on the west side of the football field.

The field orientation originated in the game's early days when games started after two o'clock in the afternoon, so the setting sun caused problems on fields oriented east-to-west. Nevertheless, fields laid out based on the available space or in existing baseball stadiums did not follow this tradition. It also became less critical in bigger stadiums with substantial stands or roofs blocking the sun.

On fields with end zones at the north and south ends, ball carriers do not gain ground by running east or west, only by running north or south. That led coaches to describe runners who hit the hole directly and seldom run parallel to the line of scrimmage as **north-south runners**. Jim Brown of Syracuse and Cleveland Browns fame was among the game's top north-south runners, but Baylor's Farrell Fisher was the first to be called a north-south runner in 1957.

Despite being praised as a north-south runner, the only picture of Fisher running
the ball in Baylor's 1958 yearbook shows him on a sweep versus Houston. (The
Texas Collection, Baylor University, Waco, Texas)

Four-Down Territory

Some football terms come onto the scene for no apparent reason despite
similar concepts being around for decades. As discussed earlier, football's
tradition and rules kept the quarterback responsible for play calling until
the middle of the twentieth century. That led coaches to use strategy
maps to teach quarterbacks how field position affected play calling,
including the decision to punt or attempt a field goal.

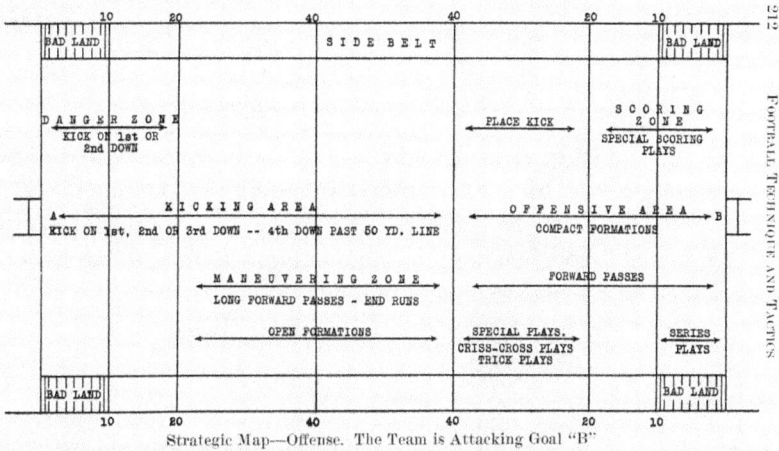

Bob Zuppke's strategy map (Zuppke, 1924)

Zuppke's map assumed his team defended the goal on the left and emphasized conservative play calling on that side of the field. It also showed punting as an option until the offense crossed the opponent's 40-yard line. That particular logic did not have a name until 1958, when Bud Wilkinson spoke at a coaching clinic:

> The aim of the offense was not to make touchdowns, but to make first downs, controlling the ball.

> If we can gain three and a half yards per play, we can keep the ball. In what we call **four-down territory** -that is, inside the opponent's 35 or 30 yard (sic) line where we're not going to punt on fourth down.[7]

The yard line at which four-down territory kicks in is team-specific and depends on the nature of the offense, the kicker's leg strength and accuracy, the wind, the game situation, and other conditions. Still, we've had a name for the area since 1958, though it is a mystery why the term did not arrive before then.

Lookout Block

When Fran Tarkenton still scrambled for the Georgia Bulldogs in 1959, reporters asked him about the conversations occurring in the team huddle. Did his teammates offer play suggestions and encouragement, or did he, as the quarterback, control the conversation? Tarkenton offered a diplomatic response, noting that the linemen often told him of opposing player weaknesses he could exploit with proper play calling.

Charley Trippi, Georgia's backfield coach at the time, interjected during the interview, saying his NFL teammates devised the **lookout block** for him: "I would get the ball and the teammate would yell, "Lookout."[8] Whether or not Trippi invented the lookout block is unclear, but he is the first credited with telling that particular tale.

Tailgating

Part of the experience of the most well-heeled fans attending early football games was dining and drinking along the sidelines from the privacy of their carriages or buggies. Newspaper accounts of the IFA championship games in New York City during the 1890s described carriages filled with fans who: "brought out their hampers as soon as they arrived on the field and those seemed to be amply provided with good things."[9]

Parking carriages along the sideline stopped being an option when stadiums grew larger and more formalized, yet the desire among fans to arrive early and have a bite to eat before the game remained. Stadiums located away from commercial areas with restaurants saw fans bring along food to consume. Yale Field, which preceded the Yale Bowl, was surrounded by open space when Harvard visited Yale in 1906. By then, it was a perfect spot for fans who arrived at games by automobile rather than horse-drawn carriage. The *New York Times* provided the first published description of what became known as a "football picnic" the following day:

> The train crowd came principally about noon. ....Each trainload as it reached the station quickly hurried away down Church Street to the campus in a mad rush to get cars to make the journey to the field. ...Few were able to get luncheon on the way, and these gazed with envious eyes as they neared the field at small parties of automobilists eating tempting viands that had been brought in hampers spread out in picnic fashion on a table cloth laid upon the ground.[10]

When steel-bodied station wagons gained popularity in the second half of the 1950s, the picnickers used their tailgates as serving tables, and **tail-**

gating replaced football picnic as the common name for the activity. In addition, tailgating received a boost from the invention of portable charcoal grills in the 1950s, allowing fans to prepare hot food onsite rather than depend solely on picnic fare.

Had His Bell Rung

Bobby Lackey, as he appeared in the 1960 Texas *Cactus* yearbook. (Texas Student Media/The Cactus)

Since the beginning, football has been a collision sport with players hitting one another and the ground, both of which present opportunities for players to hit their heads and become dizzy or concussed. Given football's long history of head injuries, it is surprising that one of the sport's favored expressions to describe these situations was late arriving.

Describing an athlete as having **had his bell rung** may have originated in boxing. Still, only one example of that connection appeared before the expression was applied to football. That came in 1959 when Texas coach Darrell Royal described his quarterback, Bobby Lackey, as having his bell rung when he was knocked unconscious against Oklahoma.

Crackback Block

As mentioned earlier, offenses began splitting their ends and sending backs in motion to spread out the defense and assist eligible receivers in releasing into pass patterns. Another reason to move players outside the bounds of close formations was to give those players better blocking angles. One version had an offensive player come from the outside to block a defender in or near the tackle box. Originally called a blindside block, it became a **crackback block** in the late 1950s, with its first use came describing the blocking of Mike Sommer, a Baltimore Colts halfback.

Gadget Play. Another name for a trick play, **gadget play** is attributed to
Sid Gillman in 1959.

9

THE NINETEEN SIXTIES

Spread, Shotgun, and Empty Formation

It is unclear whether offenses used formations that positioned players across the width of the field before 1903, but the Idaho Sweep or Idaho **Spread formation** came into use that year. Dreamed up by coach John G. Griffith, their version positioned the guards five yards wide of the center, with the tackles and ends just outside the guards. The halfback aligned behind the guards, and the quarterback and fullback were behind the guards at varying depths. The center snapped the ball across the front of his left or right leg, passing the ball to the guards or backs. Idaho continued using the formation in the first few years after the forward pass became legal in 1906, but it did not catch on elsewhere.

The spread formation began taking its modern form in the 1930s, and 1940s with Dutch Meyers and his double wing - double split end formation at TCU. There were occasional mentions of shotgun offenses in the 1940s and 1950s that presumably spread receivers like the pellets leaving a shotgun's barrel. None gained popularity.

The shotgun blossomed in 1960 under Red Sanders when the San Francisco 49ers used it to upset the Baltimore Colts. Called the **shotgun** by the 49ers, they positioned quarterback John Brodie seven yards behind the center without a running back nearby. The shotgun then lost its aim until 1975, when Tom Landry and the Dallas Cowboys revived it with Roger Staubach. It has since become football's dominant formation.

The version of the spread that does not have a running back in proximity to the quarterback became the **empty formation** with the Seattle Seahawks in 1991.

Spread - Empty Formation

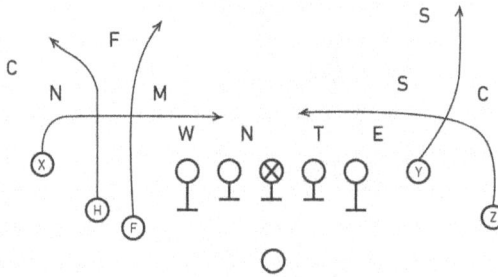

The receivers in the spread can be aligned in a variety of sets, with this example being only one version.

Passing Tree

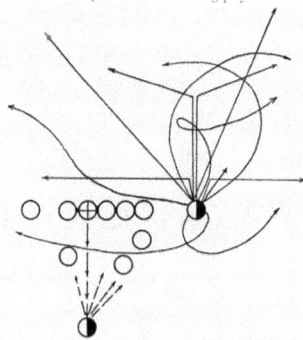

Zuppke's passing tree illustrated the available routes. He did not number the routes or refer to the illustration as a tree. (Zuppke, 1924)

As discussed previously, as offenses expanded the number of formations and plays, simply numbering plays and expecting players to memorize their responsibilities became untenable. That led coaches to name plays by their components, such as the formation, ball carrier, hole, blocking assignments, and pass routes.

Just as the ball went to a predetermined player on running plays called in the huddle, the same was true for many passing plays. In his 1924 *Football: Techniques and Tactics*, Bob Zuppke described a quarterback calling a pass play "4, 3, 6," in which the "4" designated a forward pass, the "3" indicated the halfback throws the ball, and the "6" identified the right end as the target of the pass. It is unclear how the receiver knew which route to run, but it points to passing plays and offenses being relatively simple in the 1920s, and they remained so into the 1950s.

As play variations and pass routes expanded in the 1950s, quarterbacks often named each route as part of the play call. That proved overwhelming until Don Coryell simplified things by integrating a numbered **passing tree** into his play calls.

Don Coryell, who became San Diego State's head coach in 1961, began his tenure there with an I-formation running attack. However, they struggled against superior teams, so Coryell shifted to a vertically oriented passing offense. Since Coryell recruited only junior college players into the Aztec program, he needed a simple means of teaching his complex passing scheme. He did so by numbering each route on the passing tree and using those numbers in the play calls. The simplified play call consisted of the formation, play/protection, and route numbers.

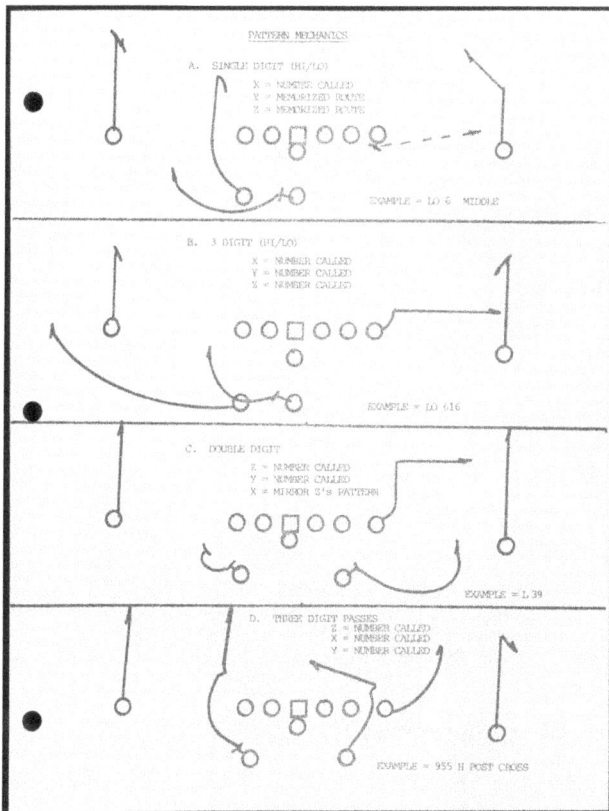

Los Angeles / San Diego Chargers route naming conventions during the 1960s when Sid Gillman was head coach. (Courtesy of the Walter Havighurst Special Collections and University Archives, Miami University Libraries, Oxford, OH)

Since only ten numbers are available on each passing tree, teams reverted to naming individual routes as needed. For example, the following shows a page from the Philadelphia Eagles playbook (circa 1980) indicating their play calls included variations of named (numbered) and memorized routes. Similar systems remain in place today at all levels of football.

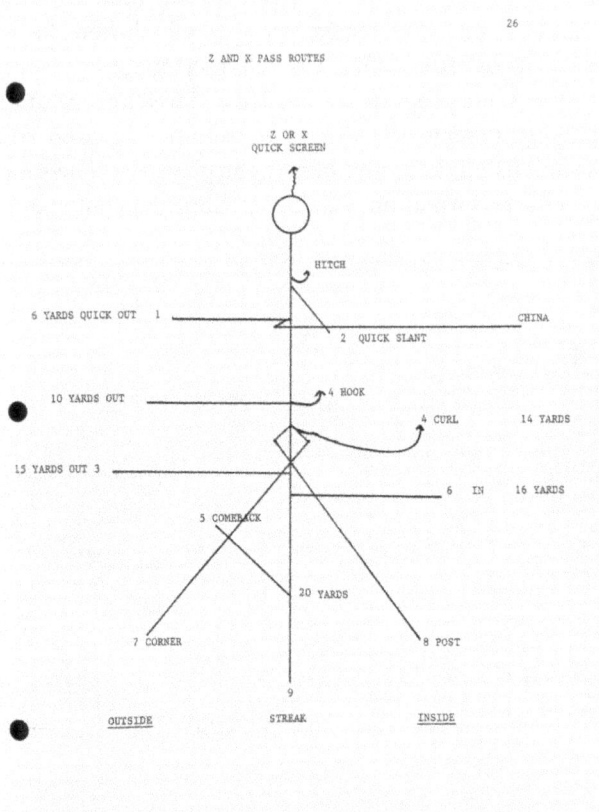

The Philadelphia Eagles' passing tree used while Sid Gillman was the QB coach from 1979 to 1981. The tree is upside down.
(Courtesy of the Walter Havighurst Special Collections and University Archives, Miami University Libraries, Oxford, OH)

Cheap Shot, Cheap Shot Artist, and Late Hit

It is appropriate that the first use of "cheap shot" in football came in Philadelphia in an October 1960 *Philadelphia News* article by Jack McKinney. McKinney wrote about Eagles linebacker Chuck Weber collecting three interceptions against the Cowboys before leaving the game following a **cheap shot** by Cowboys tackle Bob Fry.

"Cheap shot" then went silent for six weeks until the Eagles visited the Giants for a game between top NFL East teams. During the fourth quarter, Giants halfback Frank Gifford ran a drag route, caught the pass, and took several steps before Chuck Bednarik clotheslined him, causing a fumble which the Eagles recovered. Knocked unconscious, Gifford lay motionless on the field as Bednarik rose over Gifford, raising his arm in celebration of "The Hit." Gifford was hospitalized for a concussion and did not play football for another sixteen months.

Following the game, Gifford's teammate, Charlie Conerly, accused Bednarik of being a **cheap shot artist**. While Conerly's comment likely drove the increased use of the term, the iconic photo of Bednarik standing over Gifford after the hit undoubtedly contributed to the term's popularity.

The following year an undefeated Texas, led by All-American halfback Jimmy Saxton, hosted TCU in a late-season game. On the game's fifth play, Saxton caught a short pass, taking it for 45 yards before being tackled. As he quickly popped up, a trailing TCU tackle ran into Saxton, knee to head, knocking him unconscious. Despite being unable to stand for several minutes, Saxton returned to the game before being knocked out a second time. The following day's game review noted the **late hit** on Saxton. The term saw occasional use in Texas the next few years before entering the gridiron vocabulary nationwide.

Texas' James Saxton (#10) runs with the ball versus TCU. He returned to the game after being knocked unconscious by a late hit. (Texas Student Media/The Cactus, 1962 Texas Cactus)

Safety Blitz, Hot Receiver, Slant, Slant-And-Go, and Sluggo

The development of pocket pass protection in the 1950s gave quarterbacks more time to throw, forcing defenses to find new methods to confuse and pressure quarterbacks. Blitzing linebackers were not always enough, so the St. Louis football Cardinals of the early 1960s sometimes blitzed their free safety, Larry Wilson. As initially conceived, the Cardinals' **safety blitz** brought the free safety along with the three linebackers in an all-out effort to pressure the quarterback. It was a high-risk maneuver to reach the quarterback before he could get the ball to an open receiver.

A method to counter blitzes came in 1964 when Florida State's Bill Peterson had one or more receivers alter their routes to become immediate and easy targets for the quarterback, with the **hot receivers** often running routes into the area abandoned by the blitzer.

Since defenses of the time paired blitzes with man coverage, offenses also countered with quick-hitting **slant routes** made possible by quarterbacks taking the snap from under center. (In the 1940s, the slant was a common name for a T-formation fullback running off tackle. Likewise, play-action passes off the slant run were called slant passes.) By the mid-1960s, teams adapted the slant route by treating it as a fake and appending a deep or go route, creating the **slant-and-go route**. The route became a staple as a changeup in the quick-strike West Coast Offense. Bill Walsh is often credited with abbreviating slant-and-go to **sluggo**. Nonetheless, the earliest attribution is from the late 1990s, after Walsh retired as a coach.

Scrambling and Dual-Threat Quarterback and Skill Position

Jim Thorpe was the original and premier triple-threat player in the Single Wing, excelling as a runner, passer, and kicker. The Single Wing and other non-T offenses faded during the 1940s, and the Modern T brought more specialized backfield roles. One halfback became a pass-catching flanker. The fullback, often a triple-threat player in the Traditional T, took on a short-yardage running and blocking role, while the other halfback was the primary running threat.

Few expected the T quarterback to run the ball, though some showed the ability to use their legs when facing pressure. So, it was not until Fran Tarkenton's second year with the Vikings in 1962 that his ability to avoid pressure led to him being called a **scrambling quarterback**. (Previously, quarterbacks who displayed last-minute heroics were occasionally described as scramblers, but not as scrambling quarterbacks.)

A related term first appeared in 1961 before hibernating until 1966. Willamette's quarterback, Tom Lee, who played barefoot football growing up in Hawaii, was a passing and barefoot kicking threat for Willamette, leading to him being called a **dual-threat quarterback**. Other passer-kickers, such as Bob Griese, were called dual-threat quarterbacks in the 1960s, but as specialists took over kicking, "dual-threat quarterback" came to refer to those who ran and threw. Georgia's Kirby Moore led his team to the 1966 SEC championship, and Roger Staubach, playing post-Academy service football, were among the first to be called dual-threat quarterbacks.

Moore rolls out

Kirby Moore rolled out for Georgia and ran when his receivers were not open. (1967 Georgia *Pandora,* Courtesy of Hargrett Rare Book and Manuscript Library / University of Georgia Libraries.)

College football's option running game transitioned from the double option of the Split-T to the triple option veer and wishbone offenses. The core plays of each offense required the quarterback to read the defense, and give, keep, or pitch the ball. Those who ran the option well and could pass effectively also became known as dual-threat quarterbacks.

Quarterbacks who are dual threats demonstrate more than one skill, running backs and receivers are also supposed to have skills, while offensive linemen supposedly do not. That belief system led Dick Cullum, a sportswriter for the *Minneapolis Star Tribune*, to differentiate the Minnesota Gophers team of 1966 based on the line versus **skill positions**. Cullum may have picked up the term from a coach along the way, but he was the first to put that nonsense in print.

Long Snapping and Long Snapper

When snapper-backs or centers snapped with their feet, quarterbacks fielded the ball and tossed it to a fullback or halfback in punting situations. They followed the same process for some time after centers began snapping with their hands. but centers snapped to holders on placement field goal attempts starting in 1896 and to punters by the late 1890s. The Notre Dame Box and Single Wing offenses also required accurate direct snapping to backs positioned several to seven yards behind the line of scrimmage.

Nevertheless, football did not develop a term to describe snapping to a teammate positioned more than a yard or two behind the line of scrimmage until the 1940s when the Modern T and Split T offenses came along. Beginning in 1947, people distinguished snaps to quarterbacks under center from snaps to holders or punters by calling the latter **long snapping**. Likewise, those who executed those snaps were called *long ball snappers* in 1947, *long-range snapper-backs* in 1953, and finally, **long snappers** in 1961.

Dump, Sack, and Strip Sack

Since Bradbury Robinson of St. Louis University threw the first legal forward pass in 1906, many quarterbacks and others have been tackled behind the line of scrimmage while trying to throw a pass. Still, it was not until the 1930s that tackling a passer behind the line of scrimmage became known as a **dump**.

While newspapers sometimes mentioned dumps, the term saw inconsistent use, likely because football tracked few defensive statistics. The NFL did not track yardage losses until 1961, and then did not track the defensive player making the tackle. Likewise, the NFL started tracking dumps per team in the late 1960s but did not track them by player until 1982.

By 1982, however, team statisticians were the only people calling them dumps. Everyone else used the term popularized by David "Deacon" Jones of the Los Angeles Rams. As he explained:

> We needed a new term. I gave it some thought and came up with the term
> '**sack**,' like you sack a city, you devastate it. And the word was so short...
> But, wow, I never thought it would take off like that.[1]

Meanwhile, in the early 1990s, coaches, players, and writers recognized that the highest form of sack came when the defensive player stripped the ball from the passer during the sack, and so, the **strip sack** was born.

Full House T

The Modern T emerged in 1940 with two halfbacks and a fullback in line behind the quarterback and then began morphing toward the pro forma-tion. As the T became the pro formation, there came a need for the version of the T formation with both ends aligned tight and a full backfield.

Bob Devaney was coaching Wyoming in 1961, his fifth and last year there, before leaving for Nebraska. Devaney used multiple formations, including the old-fashioned Modern T, which became the **full house T**.

Instant Replay

The first implementation and use of the term "instant replay" came in 1956 when ABC implemented closed-loop systems to replay shows in different time zones. Instant replay was also a common term used in advertising for consumer tape recorders in the late 1950s and early 1960s since they allowed users to press the rewind button momentarily and "instantly replay" the recording.

The challenge for using these recording technologies in broadcasts of football games was not the ability to record the images and sound but to instantly retrieve the appropriate slice for display. CBS solved that problem and implemented it for the 1963 Army-Navy game when Army quarterback Rollie Stichweh's fourth-quarter touchdown was the first play shown using the technology. Nevertheless, the first instance of the term's use in a football context came in 1964 when San Francisco 49ers defensive back Ben Scotti complained the technology made players look bad. As Scotti said:

It's not enough that they (the fans) get to see you get beat once, now they've got to see it twice.[2]

While many of us can be sympathetic to Scotti's concern, his post-NFL career included time as a television producer, during which he co-produced the TV show *Baywatch*, so he has no right to complain about anything related to quality television.

Line Judge

The typical NFL team of the 1960s used a pro formation with a tight end, split end, and flanker. It also saw the entry of scrambling quarterbacks like Fran Tarkenton. To improve downfield monitoring while also ensuring scrambling quarterbacks were behind the line of scrimmage when throwing the ball, the NFL added the line judge, positioned on the line of scrimmage opposite the head linesman, in 1965. The line judge took over the position on the field and many responsibilities previously handled by the field judge, allowing the field judge to rejoin the back judge in the defensive backfield. College football added the line judge in 1972.

Spike the Ball

The New York Giants' Homer Jones is credited with being the first player to **spike the ball** to celebrate making a touchdown when he did so after an 89-yard pass from Earl Morrall in October 1965. Before Jones' spike, some players celebrated by throwing the football into the stands. The NFL fined players for those stunts, so Jones opted for a cheaper means of celebrating. The spike heard around the NFL was followed by the many end zone celebrations that are part of the NFL today.

Cut Block and Chop Block

Diving at or rolling through a defender's lower legs to cut him down became known as a **cut block** in the late 1930s. In the mid-1960s, however, chop block became synonymous with cut block for some, while others considered it a misunderstanding. For most, a **chop block** occurred when one offensive player, typically an offensive lineman, engaged a defender high, and an offensive lineman or back struck the defender low.

Chop blocks led to numerous leg injuries, so the NCAA and high schools banned chop blocks in 1980. The NFL allowed them in certain circumstances before banning them altogether in 2016. The cut block, executed by a single offensive player, remains legal at all levels, though its use to limited mainly to the tackle box.

Pancake Block

Offensive linemen toil in relative obscurity. None of the game's official statistics track their performance. Instead, their coaches evaluate them using grading systems assessing whether or how well they carry out their assignments each play. One unofficial measure of exceptional performance occurs when a blocker overwhelms a defender and flips him onto his back. These remarkable feats are known as **pancake blocks**.

Jim Carlen (standing in the center) and his staff at West Virginia tracked pancake blocks starting in 1966. Offensive line coach Jack Fligg stands to the far left, and offensive coordinator Bobby Bowden kneels second from right. (West Virginia and Regional History Center, WVU Libraries)

Many sources suggest the term arose to describe the work of Bill Fralic, a two-time All-America at Pitt and the second pick in the 1985 NFL draft. However, the first mentions of pancake blocks came in 1966 from Jim Carlen and his West Virginia staff, fifteen years before Fralic entered Pitt.

The West Virginia staff tracked pancake blocks after jumping on the trend of awarding helmet stickers to players meeting specific criteria. Carlen's system awarded points for deflected passes, recovered fumbles, and pancake blocks, adding a sticker to a player's helmet for every twenty points earned.

So, why did it take until the 1960s for someone to track pancake blocks? One explanation is that easing the restrictions on offensive linemen using their hands and arms made dominant blocks more frequent. More likely, however, Carlen or a staff member came up with a fun term encapsulating the block's dominance. The clever name helped it spread in the coaching network. It entered widespread awareness in the 1980s as television broadcasts increasingly used multiple cameras and instant replay to analyze the battles occurring in the trenches, allowing analysts to use the term to add color to their comments.

Triple Option, Veer, and Wishbone

The Split T was the dominant option offense in college football through the 1950s. Its option play included a predetermined fake on the dive, with the quarterback making a keep-pitch decision based on reading the defensive end. Then, in the late 1950s, Ben Schwartzwalder at Syracuse developed an outside read or ride series with two defender reads. It was the first series consistently called a **triple option**, but his version of the triple option fell out of view after 1960.

The next triple option to pop up came in 1965 with Bill Yeoman's Houston **Veer** or Split-Back Veer. As with the Split T, the offensive line used wide splits, forcing the tackles in the then-popular 5-2 defense to split wide, which gave the quarterback time to make the read. The wide splits also ensured the defensive tackle could not reach the dive back without crashing down the line. If the defensive tackle crashed, the quarterback kept the ball and continued down the line to read the defensive end, leading to a pitch to the halfback or keeping it and turning upfield.

Veer

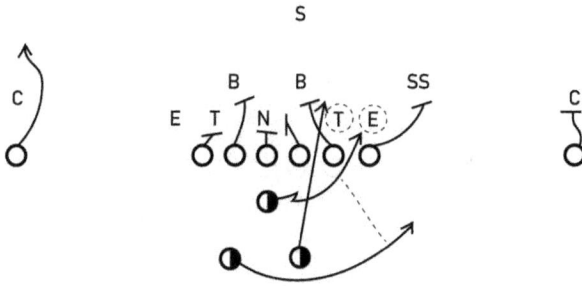

The Inside Veer had the QB read the defensive tackle for the dive and the defensive end for the pitch.

Houston set off a flurry of option activity as other schools adopted it. Then, in the summer before the 1968 season, Texas coach Darrell Royal charged his assistant coach, Emory Ballard, with devising a new offensive scheme that debuted in the season opener versus Houston. Initially called the *Y formation* or *wish-bone T*, it soon became known as the **Wishbone** or Bone. It was a triple-option attack like the Veer, but had three running backs rather than two. The fullback aligned behind the quarterback with a halfback on either side, another yard or two deep. With its core play, the Bone allowed a quick-hitting dive option in which the quarterback gave or kept the ball based on reading the unblocked defensive tackle. The quarterback then continued moving behind the line of scrimmage, reading the defensive end to determine whether to keep the ball and turn upfield or pitch to the trailing halfback.

Wishbone Lead Option

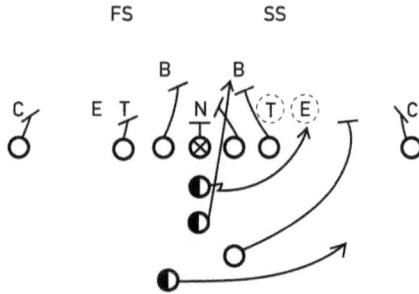

The Wishbone QB read the defensive tackle for the dive and the defensive end for the pitch on the Lead Option.

Teams running the Wishbone won seven college national championships between 1969 and 1979.

Nickel and Dime Packages

The previous chapter mentioned that "tight end" entered football's vocabulary in the late 1950s. After the Chicago Bears drafted tight end Mike Ditka, in 1961, he immediately caused problems for defensive coaches, including the Philadelphia Eagles defensive backs coach Jerry Williams. Williams modified the Eagles' 43 defense to cover Ditka by inserting a fifth defensive back in place of an outside linebacker.

George Allen copied the Eagles' five-defensive back package, calling it the **nickel** defense. While coaching the Los Angeles Rams, Allen's defensive line, the Fearsome Foursome, was able to pressure quarterbacks without the help of blitzes. That allowed Allen to extend the nickel defense to a 3-2-6 alignment or **dime** defense in 1969.

Turf Toe

ChemGrass first covered a football field in 1966 when the Astrodome hosted the Houston Cougars. Renamed AstroTurf later that year, it and other brands of artificial turf have substantially impacted the game. Early versions of synthetic turf often had inadequate padding and provided more grip than natural grass. The combination allowed players to make cuts and stop in unnatural ways. As a result, non-contact knee injuries became more common, as did a previously rare injury resulting from the pressure exerted on the big toe from quick stops. This painful toe sprain, which kept players out of action for weeks, became known as AstroTurf toe or **Turf Toe**.

Hands Team

Marv Levy had been the head coach at New Mexico, California, and William & Mary but wanted to try coaching pro football. He joined the Philadelphia Eagles coaching staff in 1969, primarily working with their special teams. (Lou Holtz replaced Levy at William & Mary.) One idea he implemented that year was creating a special kick return team that took the field only when the Eagles expected the opponent to attempt an onside side.

The unit's goal was to gain possession of the ball, not advance it, so it did not need blockers, only ball handlers. Levy stocked the unit with receivers and defensive backs since those players had the best hands on the team and called the unit the **hands team**.

Post Route. The first mention of a receiver running a **post route** came when Glen Bond of LaGrange (LA) High School did so in 1964. The next came three years later when Bob Hayes of the Dallas Cowboys mentioned he had the choice of running a post or corner route, depending on how he was defended on the play.

10

THE NINETEEN SEVENTIES

Red Zone

Back when coaches could not communicate with their teams during games, they trained their quarterbacks on play-calling strategies at various points on the field and in the game. For example, Herbert Reed, coach at Hillsdale College from 1908 to 1912, taught his quarterbacks to run or pass on fourth down rather than attempt a field goal when inside the opponent's 20-yard line.

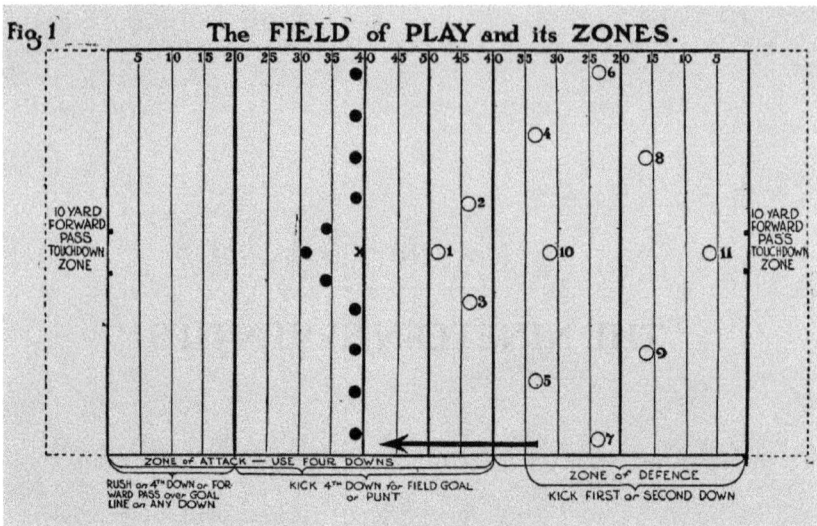

Fig. 1 — The FIELD of PLAY and its ZONES.

Reed preached the red zone concept sixty-plus years before it had a name. (Reed, 1913)

The same area became known as the **red zone**, with its first known mention coming during NBC's coverage of Super Bowl XI in 1977. NBC ran a cartoon during the game showing broadcaster Paul Maguire running through a brick wall on the 20-yard line to showcase the Cowboys' efficiency when in the red zone.

Others at the high school and NFL levels referenced the red zone in the next few years before the term exploded in use after Washington Redskins head coach Joe Gibbs focused on his red zone offense after his team struggled to score anf they started the 1982 season with an 0-4 record.

Zone Blocking

During the days when defenses aligned in one or two formations and remained in their alignments until the snap, offenses could use man or assignment blocking schemes in which each blocker was responsible for a given defender. Since defenders seldom moved pre-snap and largely drove straight ahead post-snap, assignment blocking worked, providing there was good execution.

However, as defenses increasingly used shifts, blitzes, and stunts, the location of defensive players post-snap became less predictable, forcing offenses to adapt. Many did so using **area blocking**, which made blockers responsible for lanes rather than specific defenders. Initially, area blocking was used only with pairs of offensive linemen. Bear Bryant used area blocking at Kentucky in 1951, as did Jim Tatum with Maryland in 1953. (Bryant referred to his scheme as zone blocking, but would be considered area blocking today.) Vince Lombardi also used area or "do-dad" blocking when his man-blocking schemes were problematic.

Zone blocking is area blocking on steroids. Instead of pairs of offensive linemen executing area blocks to solve local problems, the entire offensive line applies the area blocking philosophy. For example, the Green Bay Power Sweep that used man-blocking rules (down blocks combined with pull and peel guards) becomes an outside zone run with the playside offensive linemen stepping laterally before moving upfield to engage whichever lineman appears in their lane, often double teaming before one of the double teamers releases to the next level. The backside offensive linemen often cut block the backside defenders.

Zone Blocking

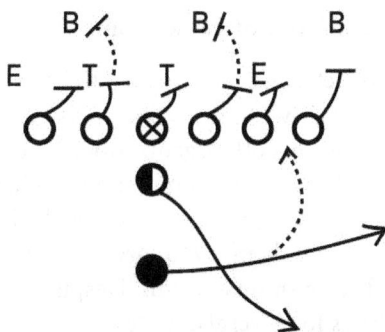

Three-, Five-, and Seven-Step Drops, Timing Route, and Yards After the Catch (YAC)

Among the innovative passing offenses of the 1960s and 1970s were those coached or influenced by Sid Gillman and Don Coryell. Both emphasized precise downfield pass route combinations that spread the receivers vertically and horizontally, mostly vertically. Meanwhile, when Bill Walsh became an assistant with the Cincinnati Bengals under Paul Brown in 1968, injuries forced the Bengals to play quarterback Virgil

Carter, who had skills but lacked superior arm strength. The Bengals adjusted by relying on shorter routes thrown more quickly, an approach that evolved into the West Coast Offense. The West Coast Offense required synching receivers' routes to the depth and timing of the quarterback's **three-, five-,** and **seven-step drops,** with all three terms entering football's vocabulary between 1972 and 1974. In addition, while coaches and players had talked about routes and timing for years, it was not until 1978 that **timing routes** entered the chat.

Walsh also stressed the need for accurate passing, hitting receivers in the chest and in stride to help them run with the ball after the catch. Although Walsh stressed the concept during his time with the San Francisco 49ers, it did not enter the general football vocabulary until 1992. At that time, the Buffalo Bills' head coach, Marv Levy, and his Defensive Coordinator, Walt Corey, spoke of their team's failure to control the 49ers' run after the catch (RAC), a term that never picked up steam. Instead, when former 49ers assistant Ray Sherman became the New York Jets Offensive Coordinator in 1994, he emphasized YAC during training camp. **Yards after catch (YAC)** soon became the preferred expression and the acronym for the NFL's official yards-after-catch statistic.

Time in Possession and Time of Possession

The NFL did not collect consistent game statistics until 1932, and the NCAA held off until 1937 (with only 70 schools participating in the first year.) After implementation, both organizations had settling-in periods to adjust the statistics and their rules. For example, Gus Dorais, who quarterbacked Notre Dame during Knute Rockne's playing days and was the University of Detroit's coach in 1940, argued for tracking each team's number of plays and **time in possession.** Despite his suggestion, neither became official statistics for several decades.

Time in possession reappeared in the mid-1960s when writers, for example, cited teams losing games despite possessing the ball 75 percent of the time. It is unclear whether the possession times were approximate or actual, though many schools tracked the time of possession in the 1970s.

The NFL began tracking the statistic in 1977 while changing the terminology changed from "time in possession" to **time of possession.** Time of possession became an official NCAA statistic in 2005.

· · ·

Cover 2 and 3, and Tampa 2

A continuing refrain is that defenses evolve with offensive innovations and vice versa. For example, the Gillman and Coryell passing offenses of the 1960s and 1970s used sets with two backs and two receivers. Defensively, teams tried to pressure quarterbacks with four defensive linemen and limited blitzing while relying on their cornerbacks to cover the wide receivers one-on-one. Meanwhile, each safety had deep zone responsibility for half the field, a general coverage shell called **Cover 2**, which first appeared in 1975.

An alternative defense turned the strong safety into a run-stopping, hybrid linebacker and made the cornerbacks and free safety responsible for deep thirds. Focused on stopping the run while taking away the threat of breakaway runs and long passes with the three deep backs, **Cover 3's** first mention came when a Chicago Bears receiver described the St. Louis Cardinals' coverage on a touchdown reception in 1977.

The defense known as **Tampa 2** developed under Tony Dungy and Monte Kiffin with the Tampa Bay Buccaneers in 1996. Considered an offshoot of Cover 2, it covered a deep middle seam by dropping the middle linebacker behind the underneath coverage and shallower than the Cover 2 safeties. Dungy often acknowledged he adapted the scheme from his playing days with the late 1970s Pittsburgh Steelers. Interestingly, while Tampa first used Tampa 2 in 1996, it did not emerge in the print media until early 2000, when Kurt Warner discussed going against the "Tampa Cover 2 defense." Shortly after that, it became widely referred to as Tampa 2 and remains active in the NFL today.

Pooch Kick

The rule restricting the kicking team from touching the punted ball inside the ten dropped from the college books in 1962, leading to another change in punting strategy. Down Arkansas way, Frank Broyles applied Red Sanders' tactic of short punts and downing the ball inside the ten, but by then, "squib kick" had come to refer to kickoffs, not punts. Broyles called his short punt a **pooch kick**, likely a bastardization of punch kick.

Just as squib kick originated as a term to describe a short punt and evolved to describe a shortened kickoff, the same occurred to the pooch kick by the mid-1970s. Today, a squib kick is a hard, low kickoff that is difficult to handle and disrupted the return team's timing.

A pooch kick, on the other hand, is a high, short kick or punt. On a kick-off, the kicking team wants a player other than the primary return man to field the kick while allowing the coverage personnel to get downfield. If executed properly, a pooch punt pins the return team deep in their territory, so it retains the original meaning of the squib kick and pooch kick.

Side Judge and Center Judge

Concerns about tight ends and other receivers being held and interfered with fifteen to twenty yards downfield led the NFL to experiment with the **side judge** during the 1977 preseason. Positioned with the field and back judges in the defensive backfield, the role became permanent in 1978. The NCAA followed suit in 1983 and one-upped the NFL by adding an eighth official, the **center judge**, to assist the referee in monitoring line play. The center judge stands behind and to the left of the offensive formation.

Flak Jacket

Pads to protect the ribs have been around since at least the 1930s. Called blocking pads because they protected the ribs of backs and ends that executed body or rolling blocks, they used the same materials as the shoulder pads and hip pads of the time: leather or fiber over felt or foam rubber pads.

While blocking offered some protection for healthy players, they were less effective for players already suffering from sore or broken ribs. The lack of adequate rib protection became more problematic as quarterbacks increasingly threw from the pocket, leaving themselves vulnerable to being hit in the ribs.

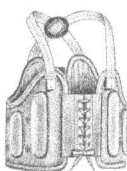

No. 139   No. 15X

No. 135

GoldSmith *Preferred* Blocking Pads

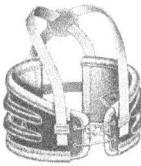

No. 132

No. 139—Form fitting, made of 9-oz. duck, well padded and stiffened with protective curved fibre. Heavy elastic connectors at front and back with leather lacers and metal eyelets. Adjustable web suspenders. Eyeleted for ventilation. Sizes: Large, Medium and Small .... Each, $5.15

No. 15X—Jointed fibre covered with khaki and padded with 100% pure Kapok. Adjustable elastic front strap with snap fastener, elastic back, web suspender .... Each, $4.45

No. 135 —"Airlite" cushion rubber padding encased in white drill faced on outside with "turtle-back" molded fibre. Adjustable wide elastic laced connector at back, single elastic web strap in front. Adjustable web suspenders .... Each, $4.35

No. 132—Heavy gauge molded corrugated fibre with tapered front padded with "Airlite" cushion rubber and covered with white drill. Top and bottom edges of fibre padded with white felt. Elastic web strap at back, laced front. Adjustable suspender straps. Regular and large sizes. Sizes: Large and Medium .... Each, $4.00

No. 130

No. PV4

No. PV2

No. 130—Heavy gauge molded corrugated fibre padded with thick soft rubber, with edges padded at top and bottom with felt. Elastic web strap at back, laced front. Adjustable suspender straps .... Each, $3.35

No. 127—Light weight molded corrugated curved fibre padded on upper and lower edges with light weight felt. Adjustable web suspender straps, elastic back, laced front .... Each, $2.35

PROTECTOR VESTS

No. PV4—Made of fine quality white airp'ane cloth "Airlite" cushion rubber padding in back of neck. Corrugated fibre protection over ribs padded on inside and outside with Kapok felt. Eyelets for lacing to shoulder pad. Sizes: Small (36-38), Medium (40-42), Large (44-46) .... Each, $6.35

No. PV2—Made of white airplane cloth. "Airlite" cushion rubber padding in back of neck. Vertical fibre protection over ribs. Eyelets for lacing to shoulder pad. Sizes: Small (36-38), Medium (40-42), Large (44-46) .... Each, $6.35

No. 127

ALL PURPOSE BRUISE PADS

Made of curved fibre with "Airlite" cushion rubber padded edges. Three sizes.
No. F3—9½-inches long .... Each, $ .75
No. F2—7½-inches long .... Each, .60
No. F1—5½-inches long .... Each, .45

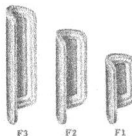

F3   F2   F1

— 23 —

Blocking pads available in the 1940 GoldSmith Preferred Sports
Equipment Fall & Winter catalog.

Little changed with rib-protecting equipment until playoff-bound Houston Oilers quarterback Dan Pastorini suffered three broken ribs in a late-season game in 1978. Afterward, as Pastorini sat in a hospital bed, two unauthorized men stepped into Pastorini's room. One, named Byron Donzis, wore a padded vest and raised his arms over his head while the other man struck Donzis in the ribs with a baseball bat. Donzis did not flinch, which convinced Pastorini that a similar vest might serve him well.

The **flak jacket** provided enough protection that Pastorini played in a wildcard game several weeks later, and the win took the Oilers to the AFC Championship game.

Drag Route. A drag route is an "in route' with the receiver cutting to the inside approximately five yards downfield and continuing across the formation. Receivers can adjust the route's depth and path based on the linebackers' location. The term first appeared in 1970.

Seam Route. While most pass routes involve specific movements and direction changes, seam routes are defined by being run on the borders of the zones between defenders. The term likely originated at Oklahoma since several of the first mentions come from Sooner staff members in 1974.

Fade Route. Receivers positioned on or outside the field numbers sometimes run what appears to be a go route before fading to the sideline or end zone corner. The quarterback throws the ball high and outside, so the intended receiver makes the catch or the ball goes out of bounds. This tactic has been called a **fade route** since 1978.

11

THE NINETEEN EIGHTIES

Flex Tight End, H-Back, and Inline Tight End

When offenses first split their ends in the 1920s, they aligned a few yards or more from the tackles but did not dramatically alter their offense. Similarly, after moving to pass-friendly offenses, teams that retained a tight end, sometimes split them several yards from the tackle. Maryland, for example, did so in 1971, referring to the tactic as the **flex tight end**.

As teams moved to one-back or spread formations in the 1980s, some opted to employ tight ends who were capable blockers but with high-end route running and pass-catching abilities whose size caused matchup problems for defensive backs. Players with those skills, such as Jay Novacek of the Dallas Cowboys (drafted in 1983), redefined the flex tight end role in football.

During the 1980 season, Joe Gibbs' was in his third season as the San Diego Chargers' Offensive Coordinator under Don Coryell when he implemented the one-back offense to deal with the outside linebackers dominating the game. The one-back involved swapping a running back for a tight end-like player who aligned in multiple locations and shifted frequently.

Gibbs became the Redskins head coach the next year. When diagramming plays, he labeled the quarterback the Q, the fullback the F, and the half-back the H, and the fullback was the F. Since John Riggins was the team's best running back, he (an F) became the one-back in the offense, so H designated the flexible tight end, a role that became known as the **H-Back**. Still, it was not until 1983, when Gibbs' assistant, Dan Henning, became the Atlanta Falcons head coach and publicly discussed the plans for his offense, that H-Back spilled into the public discussion.

While the flex tight end or H-Back was pass-friendly, teams continued using tight ends whose skill set leaned toward blocking from close formations. Sometimes called an "in-line blocking tight end," they became **in-line tight ends** when the Cowboys' Bill Parcells adopted the term in 2003.

Progression Read

Into the 1960s, it was not uncommon for passing offenses to send only two receivers downfield, one on each side, so determining if or which receiver was open was simple. The passer's choices remained limited even when three receivers went downfield; they looked for an open receiver and threw him the ball.

More sophisticated coverages and the advent of spread formations with four or five receivers increased the quarterback's options, which required tools to prioritize those options.

That prioritization typically occurred based on the quarterback identifying the defense via pre-snap reads and the initial reactions of key defenders. Then, given the defense and the play called, the quarterback determined whether a designated receiver was open. If not, he progressed to receiver number two and then to receiver number three.

This process became known by the early 1980s as a progression read or progression of reads. The term's first appearance came in a quote by Marc Wilson, a second-year quarterback for the Oakland Raiders. Ironically, despite their use of progression reads, the Raiders set an NFL record that season by being shut out three times.

Smash Route

Offensive play calling became more difficult as defenses disguised or switched their coverage just before or after the snap. The last-second nature of the defensive switching meant audibles did not solve the problem. Instead, offenses reacted by developing option routes that had the receivers change their pattern based on reading the defense as executed.

An example route or concept of this type is the smash route, a combination of routes run by two receivers on the same side, first referenced in 1982 by the Cincinnati Bengals. The core smash route has the outside receiver run a 5 to 6-yard hitch before gliding toward the sideline. The base route for the inside receiver is a 12-yard corner route. However, based on the cornerback's action and position, the inside receiver might execute a hook or flatten the corner route. Ideally, the quarterback reads the defense like the outside receiver, throws the ball on time, and to the spot where the receiver is open.

Field, Boundary, and Shutdown Corner

Hash marks play a significant role in football, sometimes affecting the design of defenses and related terminology. But not all hash marks are created equal since high school hash marks divide the field into thirds, the NFL hash marks align with the goal posts, and college hash marks fall between the two. That results in high school and college defenses often having much more space to defend to the ball's right or left than in the other direction.

Differences in the space to defend and offensive tactics led some coaches to adjust their defenses and personnel. For example, since the cornerback nearest the sideline had less room to defend than the cornerback on the other side, he became known as the closed, closed-side, or **boundary cornerback**. His counterpart, who required more speed and one-on-one coverage skills, became the open side, open, wide-field, wide, or **field cornerback**.

The earliest discussion of these concepts related to Ohio State's two-time All-American Jack Tatum during the 1970 season. Varying terminology floated around for fifteen years before field and boundary cornerback in combination showed up at USC in 1985.

A related term appeared in the mid-1990s to describe cornerbacks so talented they could eliminate or minimize the impact of the opponent's best receiver. First mentioned in 1996 in a week one summary noting that the San Francisco 49ers lacked a **shutdown corner**, the first player to be given the designation was Northern Arizona's Samaji Akili.

• • •

Bull Rush

Beginning in the early 1890s, players spoke, and writers wrote of tough runners who ran the ball up the middle, shedding would-be tacklers through toughness and force of will. Teams like Yale were known to power the ball down the field with their ball carriers "bull rushing" through defenses. Jim Taylor, a Hall of Fame fullback with the Lombardi-era Packers, was among the last runners known to bull rush before the term fell from use in the 1970s.

Bull rush reemerged in the 1980s as the preferred term for the technique used by defensive linemen and linebackers attempting to run through a pass blocker, overpowering him and putting the blocker on their heels through power and leverage.

Hurry Up and No Huddle Offense

As mentioned earlier, football's pace of play in the game's first decades resembled that of rugby. A play ended, the teams lined up, called the signals at the line, and they snapped the ball. Things moved quickly, yet some moved quicker than others. John Heisman claimed his 1899 Auburn team was exceptionally speedy, often catching slow-moving opposing players behind the line of scrimmage. During the same season, Fielding "Hurry Up" Yost famously instructed his quarterback at Kansas, Bennie Owens, to start calling plays while still on the ground after being tackled. **Hurry up offense** first appeared in 1902 in a discussion of its use by a high school in Green Bay.

The hurry-up approach continued popping up over the years, gaining significant attention following Oklahoma's 1956 Orange Bowl victory over Maryland. The Sooners sped up the pace by hustling back to the huddle, quickly calling the play, running to the line of scrimmage, and snapping the ball. Like Auburn and Kansas more than fifty years earlier, Oklahoma executed routine processes but did so faster than the norm.

Another form of the hurry-up is the **no-huddle offense**, which has been around since St. Mary's ran it in the 1930s. Early no-huddlers typically ran one play or one series at a time. The offense had a single play or short series of plays scripted to run when the quarterback sensed the defense was napping. Geneva College ran a no-huddle offense in the early 1960s, with every play called via audible at the line of scrimmage. Various colleges used this approach in the 1960s and 1970s, running the no-huddle for most or all of some games.

The most recent version arrived in 1984 when Sam Wyche implemented the no-huddle with the Cincinnati Bengals to keep defenses from making situational substitutions. The Bengals moved to the no-huddle full-time in 1988. Their version of the no-huddle offense also eliminated the quarterback's role in communicating the play by calling them from the sideline via hand signals or images on signs.

Icing the Kicker

The kicker's job is to send the ball through the uprights on each field goal and extra point attempt. The opposing team's job is to block the kick or distract the kicker, leading to a miss The current favorite method of distracting the kicker today is the opposing coach calling a timeout shortly before the kicker attempts the kick, a tactic once considered poor sportsmanship.

The first identified instance of an opposing team calling a timeout before a late kick attempt came when Michigan State did so versus Iowa in 1969. As it turned out, Iowa's Al Scheutte made the extra point attempt with 1:25 left in the game, and the Hawkeyes hung on for a 19-18 victory. There were occasional mentions during the 1970s of opposing coaches calling time out to "make the kicker think," but the tactic went nameless.

The expression, **icing the kicker** appeared in 1985 when Purdue called a timeout before Iowa's kicker, Rob Houghtlin, kicked a 25-yard field goal with 1:08 left. Although the tactic seemingly had just acquired a name, the reporter mentioned that the tactic was so common it was losing its effect:

> Trying to ice the place-kicker with a timeout is such a cliché these days, such a common practice, the tactic has probably outlived it's (sic) effectiveness.[1]

Icing's logical conclusion came following a 2004 NFL rule change that allowed coaches to call timeouts from the sideline. (Previously, only players on the field could call a timeout). Denver Broncos coach, Mike Shanahan, leveraged the new rule in 2007 by calling a timeout a split second before the kicking team snapped the football. As it turned out, the

Oakland Raiders' Sebastian Janikowski famously made the disallowed attempt and then missed the shot that counted.

Personnel Grouping or Package

For the first twenty-plus years after football moved to unlimited substitutions, coaches relied on their starters to win games, inserting substitutes here and there. In 1975, however, the Dallas Cowboys under Tom Landry revived the spread formation with Roger Staubach running it on third down and in two-minute drills. Landry's use of the spread on third downs foreshadowed offensive **personnel groupings** or packages, a term first expressed by Sam Wyche in 1985. Defenses had used personnel groupings since the onset of nickel and dime defenses in the 1960s, and the Cincinnati Bengals had a "Bear" package in 1985, but they did not refer to them as personnel grouping

The next step in the language of personnel groupings came as offenses increased their situational substitutions and needed a method to quickly communicate the personnel required on the field for each play. In the late 1990s, teams began identifying their offensive personnel packages using the two-digit designation seen in the following table. The first digit identifies the number of running backs on the field and the second digit represents the number of tight ends. The combination of running backs, tight ends, and wide receivers must equal five, so the wide receiver numbers are unstated. (Note: Multiple formations can be run from one grouping or package, so the two are related but distinct concepts.)

Grouping	RBs	TEs	WRs
00	0	0	5
01	0	1	4
02	0	2	3
10	1	0	4
11	1	1	3
12	1	2	2
13	1	3	1
20	2	0	3
21	2	1	2
22	2	2	1
23	2	3	0

Get Back Coach

Over the years, the NFL and NCAA attempted to control the coaches and players on the sideline. Initially, they focused on limiting coaching from the sideline and keeping players seated on the bench. However, those rules went away by the 1970s, resulting in players and others standing so close to the sideline they interfered with officials or chain gangs. Both organizations soon designated areas for players and coaches to avoid while the ball was in play, but players still crept into those zones.

Recognizing the need to remind players to stand away from the sideline, Houston Oilers and New Orleans Saints coach Bum Phillips had a non-coaching friend, Paul "Chief" Salazar, patrol the sidelines telling offenders to "Get Back." It is unclear when Salazar became Phillips' **Get Back Coach**, but his description of the role first appeared in print in 1986.

Close Line Play, Free Blocking Zone, Blocking Zone, and Tackle Box

The chapter regarding the Twenties discussed how clipping became illegal in 1920 as part of an expanded definition of unnecessary roughness. Clipping was redefined two years later to focus on striking an opponent from behind and below the knees, with the rule mentioning that it did not apply to "**close line play.**" Though close line play did not receive a formal definition until 1950, it was understood to mean the area within two or three yards of the line of scrimmage and between the offensive ends, both of whom typically aligned close or tight. As the offensive ends began splitting out over the next few decades, close line play morphed to mean from tackle to tackle.

In 1981, the high school rules federation made blocking below the waist illegal everywhere on the field except in the **free blocking zone**, while the NCAA referred to the same area as the **blocking zone** in 19xx. Both were terminological changes with no difference in application.

Things became confused in 1993, however, when the NFL adopted a rule allowing quarterbacks to throw the ball away when located outside the **tackle box**. The tackle box covers the area within five yards of the snapper and extends from the offensive line of scrimmage to the end line behind the offense. While related to one another, the blocking zone and tackle box are distinct concepts that are often confused with one another.

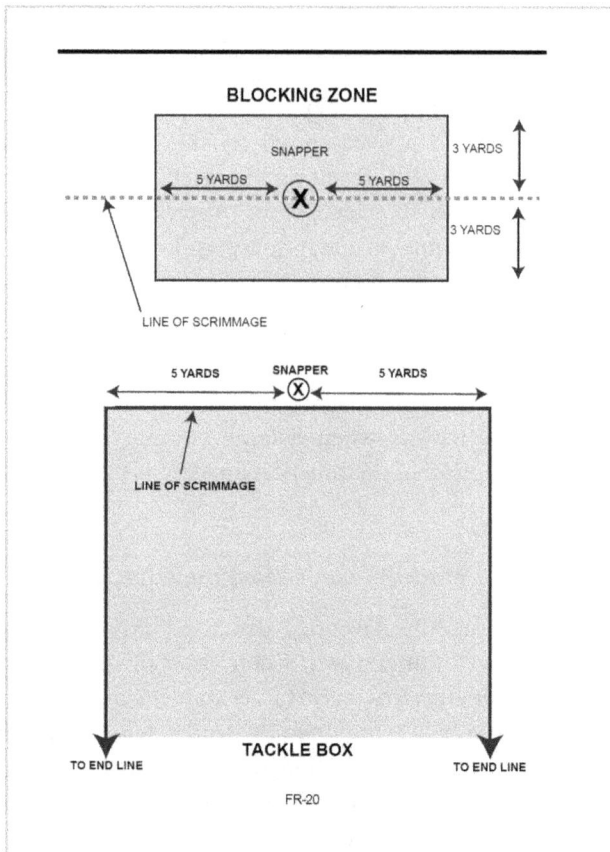

The 2009-2010 NCAA rule book included helpful diagrams
distinguishing the blocking zone and the tackle box. (2009-2010
NCAA Football Rules and Interpretations)

Jet Motion and Jet Sweep. Although flankers or slotbacks may have motioned across the formation and received a handoff before sweeping wide in the 1960s or 1970s, the play was first called a **jet sweep** in 1980. **Jet motion** appears in print several years later.

Wheel Route. The first time **wheel route** appeared in print came when Jimmy Johnson, then head coach at Oklahoma State, commented that Missouri had success with both running backs and tight ends running the route in their 1982 game.

12

THE NINETEEN NINETIES AND BEYOND

Bunch Formation and Bubble Screen

The chapter on the 1890s cited the Minnesota Shift as a tactic teams used to move into an unbalanced line formation. The Minnesota Shift had all but the center grouped behind the line of scrimmage pre-shift, so some football coaches in the 1920s sometimes referred to it as the bunch formation. Other formations and tactics earned the same description over the years.

A formation and play used by West Virginia in the mid-1910s resemble a modern bubble screen. (Publishers Syndicate, Metzger, Sol, 'West Va. Lateral Pass Aid to Maine,' *Boston Globe,* September 11, 1929.)

A West Virginia formation of the mid-1910s was an early example of a pass-oriented formation with three eligible receivers grouped wide of the offensive tackle to enable a lateral or pass to one of the three wide men. However, West Virginia's formation saw only limited use until 1992 when the Washington Redskins, under Joe Gibbs, grouped Art Monk, Ricky Sanders, and a running back well outside the offensive tackle in what they called a **bunch formation**. Five years later, the Purdue Boilermakers under Joe Tiller used a similar formation to run **bubble screens**, with the innermost of the receivers receiving a pass on a quick swing route as the other bunch receivers blocked for him.

. . .

Trickeration

Among the odder words to enter the language of football is **trickeration**, and the walk it took to enter the game is equally unusual. Trickeration originated with the release of Cab Calloway's 1931 *Trickeration*, a song about Harlem's jazz and dance scene. Best as I can tell from the lyrics, trickeration referred to musical and dance tricks that produced joy or fun. Except for trickeration being used to describe the pitching of the White Sox's Guy Bush in 1932, trickeration stayed in the musical world for the next four decades.

Its big break came in the mid-1970s through the creative language of boxing promoter Don King, who handled the "Thrilla in Manila" and the "Rumble in the Jungle." King regularly accused business adversaries of misdeeds or trickeration, despite being charged with the same.

After King faded from the sports scene, trickeration entered the football world not through coaches or players but via newspaper columnists of the mid-1990s when they slipped the word into descriptions of football financial or other maneuverings (e.g., the Raiders' nomadic treks).

Columnists then used the term to describe trick plays or offenses that used misdirection and trickery. It was not until 2007 that a coach, Brian Kelly, was quoted using trickeration to describe a play or opponent.

Physicality

It is difficult to determine when some football terms took on their current meaning, and physicality is one of them. Physicality appeared before the 1960s in Christian Science writings distinguishing the spiritual and physical.

One article from 1969 mentioned the physicality of Kansas State's football team, using the term as used today. However, for the next thirty years, the term was used in more theoretical discussions of the game, particularly when comparing it to other sports or activities. For instance, Dave Meggyesy, author of *Out of Their League*, described how his experiences in pro football caused him to lose the "intrinsic joy of physicality." Former football players turned actors also used the term to describe the roughness of the game and the bodily awareness that transferred to the stage.

Using physicality to describe a team or player that possesses (or needs to develop) toughness and power versus speed and skill grew in use in the 1990s but exploded after 2010, with mentions growing nearly tenfold from one period to the next.

Edge Rusher

After the two-platoon system entered football, those playing end on defense became known as defensive ends, and that remains their primary position description today. However, the continued advance of the passing game led to changes on the defensive side, including some defensive ends specializing in pressuring the passer rather than defending the run. These pass-rushing specialist players were called **edge rushers,** first applied to Al Noga when playing at Hawaii in 1985. A Rutgers player was called an edge rusher in 1992, and the term entered the mainstream later in the 1990s.

Spread Option, Read Option, and Zone Read

Rich Rodriguez was the head coach at Glenville State in 1994 when his quarterback kept the ball on a broken play and ran around the end after seeing the backside defensive end pinch inside to pursue the running back. Rodriguez recognized the play's potential and turned the mistake into the game's most popular option play. Run from the shotgun with one running back, the play uses zone blocking with the backside end or linebacker left unblocked. If the unblocked defender stays home, the quarterback gives the ball to the running back. Alternatively, when the defender pursues the running back, the quarterback keeps and runs through the spot abandoned by the defender.

The play became known as the **spread option** or **read option** in the late 1990s, while **zone read** first appeared in print when Vince Young began running the play at Texas in 2003.

Zone Read

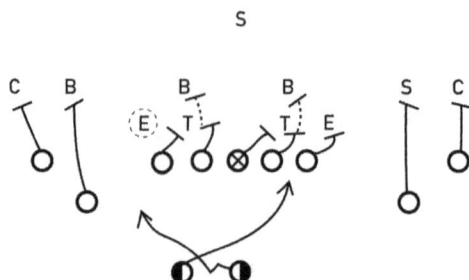

The zone read is run from a spread formation and is based on a backside read rather than the frontside read of previous option plays.

G.O.A.T. (Greatest of All Time)

The abbreviation G.O.A.T. came to national prominence in 2000 with the release of LL Cool J's album of the same name. Its first connection to football came in a 2001 article about Tom Brady as a second-year pro stepping in for the injured Drew Bledsoe. Of course, the article did not identify Brady as the G.O.A.T. Instead, it described Earl Morrall as the G.O.A.T. backup due to his stepping in for the injured Johnny Unitas in 1968, playing the entire season, and leading the Baltimore Colts to Super Bowl IV.

Morrall moved to the Miami Dolphins in 1972 and took over quarter-backing duties when Bob Griese went down in the season's fifth game. With Morrall under center, the Dolphins won their remaining nine regular season games, the Divisional Round and AFC Championship games, before Griese returned to start Super Bowl VII.

Run-Pass Option (RPO)

Among the more difficult terms to tease out its origins is the run-pass option, partly because the term has had multiple meanings that overlapped in use. "Run-pass option" came into use in the late 1940s to describe the halfback or quarterback's option to throw a pass when sweeping the end. That use of the term continued well into the first part of the 2000s and likely beyond that point.

At the same time, coaches recall using RPO logic on a limited basis in the 1990s, with quarterbacks reading specific defenders to determine whether to run or throw a bubble screen or hitch. However, those coaches did not refer to such plays as run-pass options until the early 2000s. It was not until 2015 that the abbreviation RPO came into use as shorthand for the run-pass option.

Zone Read RPO

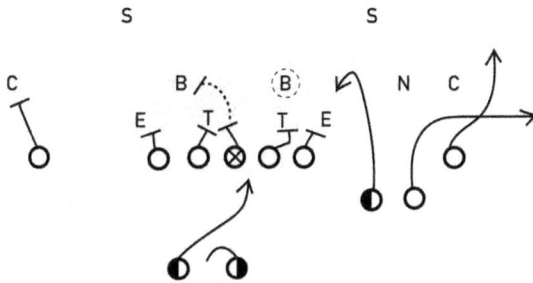

The QB reads the strong-side linebacker on this RPO. If the backer drops into coverage, the QB gives to the running back. If the backer steps up, the QB passes to the Y.

Medical Tent

Images captured by Matthew Brady and others documented how military medicine used tents during the Civil War. At the same time, episodes of the television show M*A*S*H reminded us of their use during the Korean War. Medical tents have been everyday items at triathlons, marathons, and other thons for decades. Still, they were absent from football fields until 2015, when Alabama's head trainer, Jeff Allen, conceived of and led the design of the SidelinER tent.

A SidelinER medical tent stands ready for a game at Alabama. (Courtesy of Kinematic Sports)

Allen wanted the ability to examine players while ensuring their privacy during the exam. So, working with several Alabama engineering students, they developed a popup tent with a limited footprint that fit an exam table and other essential equipment. Alabama first used its medical tent in 2015, and the tents quickly spread to football fields across the country.

Orbit Motion. Like various motions originating in the Wing-T, orbit motion involves a perimeter receiver such as slot, flanker, wing, or H-Back motioning from an outside position into the offensive backfield. The motion man's position at the snap varies based on the formation and play call. Orbit motion came over the horizon in 1999.

Back Shoulder Throw. Some argue that quarterbacks deliberately threw passes to their receivers' back shoulders as early as the 1970s. Still, the earliest reports located about such throws are from the mid-to-late 1990s, and **back shoulder throw** first appeared in print in 2002.

Mesh Route. First mentioned in 2005, **mesh routes** occur when receivers from the right and left run drag routes, crossing one another's paths over the middle. Often run against man coverage, mesh routes attempt to get the defenders covering each receiver to run into or force one another to alter their paths and lose touch with the receiver.

EPILOGUE

This book was not intended to make grand pronouncements about football but to document when and why its vocabulary emerged. Generally, the research showed that new terms generally came into public use shortly after a new tactic or approach was created, though some experienced extended delays.

Football's early vocabulary largely came from rugby, and many of those core terms remain with us today, even as we altered their meaning. For example, while onside and offside have different definitions in football, rugby, and soccer, each concerns one team possessing the ball and the players' location relative to the ball, though each defines it differently. Tackle, halfback, and fullback are also used in all three sports though their meanings have morphed over time. Those transitions stemmed from different rule makes and the physical distance, like the differences in English spoken in Manchester, Sydney, and Tuscaloosa.

Besides rugby, the most common source of football terms has been the military, though its contribution primarily came before WWI. Early discussions of football strategy often connected the game to the military and used expressions such as offense, defense, flanking, and point of attack. Among those who brought a military perspective to football was Lorin F. Deland, a play design contributor for Harvard and co-author of *Football* with Walter Camp in 1896. Although Deland was not a military man, he was a student of military history and saw the game through that lens. Other influential coaches with significant military connections included Paul Dashiell, Charles Daly, and Frank Kavanaugh. Later, Bob Neyland and Earl Blaik continued the tradition as shock troops, bombs, and blitzes entered the game.

Beyond these key coaches, however, many universities had cadet corps that influenced its member and campus life generally, while state militia and National Guard service exposed others to military thinking and terminology. Of course, the country's mobilization during WWI and WWII exposed most college-age males to military training. During both wars, football was positioned as the best training ground for young men to prepare themselves physically and mentally for war, further linking the two.

Football became an increasingly specialized and technical game after WWII, and much of the new vocabulary reflects that trend. Left and right ends who knew their place transformed into wideouts, wide receivers, X, Y, Z, and H-Backs that align in bunches or not. An entirely new defensive vocabulary emerged in the 1950s and beyond. Defensive halfbacks became safeties of various sorts, and cornerbacks of the boundary, field, and shutdown varieties now play a host of coverages, only one or two of which existed a few decades ago.

Notably, whereas football's language creation occurred on college campuses before WWII, it shifted to the professional leagues after the war. The passing game, which now dominates football, had its most significant developments in the NFL and AFL. Few college teams had pro-caliber quarterbacks, and the college rules did not favor the passing game, as did NFL rules. Pro coaches and players, with nothing better to do, dramatically increased the variations and complexity of the passing game, giving us more routes than fit on a tree, drops with different numbers of steps, along with reads, progressions, and run-pass options. Of course, college football also played a role in football knowledge creation.

Another interesting aspect of football terminology involves the number of terms that emerged only after an alternate approach entered the game. For example, the terms "straight-ahead" and "conventional-style" kickers did not exist until "soccer-style" kickers arrived in sufficient numbers that people needed terms to distinguish the styles. Similar situations occurred with:

- Single Wing followed the arrival of the Double Wing
- Single Platoon entered the conversation with Two Platoon
- Long Snapper showed up after the Hands Under Center snap

Still, the language of football is not entirely technical. Players, coaches, and media members contribute colorful expressions, often analogies for on-the-field events. Players run north and south, sack quarterbacks, hear footsteps, have their bell rung, earn pancake blocks, show a little trickeration, and become the G.O.A.T.

Whether technical or metaphoric, each word or expression contributes to our understanding and enjoyment of football. As the game continues exploring new concepts and techniques, its vocabulary will evolve and reshape how we think and talk about the game.

NOTES

1. In The Beginning

1. 'The Rugby Game at Football,' *Leeds Mercury (Yorkshire, England)*, October 6, 1870.
2. Rule 4: Each goal shall be composed of two upright posts exceeding 11 feet in height from the ground and placed 18 feet 6 inches apart, with a cross-bar 10 feet from the ground.
3. Davis, Parke H. *Football: The American Intercollegiate Game*. New York: Charles Scribner's Sons, 1911.
4. Davis, Parke H. *Football: The American Intercollegiate Game*. New York: Charles Scribner's Sons, 1911.

2. The Eighteen Nineties

1. 'Harvard's Easy Win,' *Chicago Tribune*, December 1, 1893.
2. 'Football And War,' *Pittsburgh Dispatch*, November 29, 1991.
3. Dawin, Charles. *The Voyage of the Beagle*. New York: D. Appleton. 1871.
4. Camp, Walter and Lorin F. Deland. *Football*. Houghton, Mifflin, Boston. 1896.
5. Rice, Grantland, 'Rice Pays Fine Tribute to Man of Notre Dame,' Montana Standard (Butte), April 1, 1931.
6. 'From Yale's Standpoint,' *New York Times*, November 16, 1890.
7. 'Yale Team Improved,' *New York Sun*, November 17, 1895.
8. 'A Novel Device,' *St. Louis Post-Dispatch*, November 10, 1889.
9. 'Officials for the Game,' *Boston Globe*, November 24, 1894.
10. 'Save Their Game,' *Chicago Tribune*, March 31, 1895.

3. The Nineteen Aughts

1. 'Kalamazoo,' Detroit Free Press, October 9, 1904.
2. 'Coach Kennedy Blames Defeat On Lack of Concentrated Action,' *Chicago Tribune*, November 4, 1900.
3. 'Football,' *Minneapolis Journal*, November 15, 1900.
4. 'Holds Iowa Even,' *Inter Ocean (Chicago)*, November 30, 1900.
5. Camp, Walter. Spalding's Athletic Library How to Play Football. American Sports Publishing - New York. 1904.
6. Davis, Parke H. Football the American Intercollegiate Game
7. 'Football Notes,' *Boston Globe*, October 17, 1910.

4. The Nineteen Teens

1. 'Clubs Fete Three Alton Grid Squads,' Alton Evening Telegraph IL), December 6, 1935.
2. 'Yale Star Here With U. Juniors,' *Tacoma Times*, October 23, 1915.
3. Littig, Victor L. 'Fundamental Football Comes Back To Stay In Colleges, Says Littig,' *Daily Times (Davenport, IA)*, October 18, 1916.

5. The Nineteen Twenties

1. Casey, Eddie, 'The Forward Pass Defense,' *Charlotte News*, October 28, 1920.
2. W.F.L., 'Stanford "Outside the Law," East Threatens Injunctions,' *San Francisco Examiner*, December 26, 1928.
3. 'Peabody Upsets Central Hi With Long Aerial Bomb,' *Tennessean (Nashville)*, November 28, 1929.
4. Camp, Walter. *Spalding's Athletic Library How to Play Football*. American Sports Publishing - New York. 1920.
5. Game Maxims of Coach Robert R. Neyland. Accessed October 12, 2022 in https://volo pedia.lib.utk.edu/entries/game-maxims-of-coach-robert-r-neyland/

6. The Nineteen Thirties

1. 'Two Good Games Booked Saturday,' Evening Star (Washington, D.C.), October 29, 1914.

7. The Nineteen Forties

1. Foot-Ball Rules and Referee's Book. American Intercollegiate Association. Boston-Wright & Ditson. 1888.
2. Faurot, Don. *Football: Secrets of the "Split T" Formation*. New York: Prentice-Hall, 1950.
3. Bible, Dana X. *Championship Football: A Guide for Player, Coach, Fan*. New York: Prentice-Hall. 1947.
4. *Northwestern Favored for 'Granddaddy of Them All." Town Talk* (Alexandria, LA), *January 1, 1949.*

8. The Nineteen Fifties

1. Tobin, Jack, 'Intricate Signal System Rough on Pro Quarters,' *Mirror News (Los Angeles)*, August 17, 1954.
2. Wynn, Jim, 'Wynning Ways,' *Town Talk (Alexandria, LA)*, November 30, 1957.
3. Associated Press, 'Hayes Talks At Clinic,' *Herald-News (Passaic, NJ)*, March 17, 1959.
4. Koffman, Jeff, 'Along Sport Row,' *Ottawa Citizen*, September 6, 1955.
5. Wolf, Al. 'Sportraits,' *Los Angeles Times*, December 8, 1955.
6. Strange, Mike. 'Vols Must Regain 'Alligator Arms' Defense, Steele Says,' *Knoxville News-Sentinel*, November 5, 1987.
7. Smith, Red, 'Views of Sport,' *San Bernardino County Sun*, June 27, 1958.
8. Thomey, Al. 'Quarterback's In Command, That Huddle… Why It's Not Always All Seriousness,' *Atlanta Constitution*, October 1, 1959.
9. 'The Game,' *Evening World (New York)*, November 30, 1893.
10. 'A Football-Mad Throng,' *New York Times*, November 25, 1906.

9. The Nineteen Sixties

1. Preston, Mike, 'The Sack Attack,' *Baltimore Sun*, December 21, 1988
2. Jackaubowsky, Jack. 'Between the Lines, Redwood City Tribune (CA), October 1, 1964.

11. The Nineteen Eighties

1. Turnbull, Buck, 'Hawkeyes Survive Purdue Scare, 27-24,' *Des Moines Register*, October 17, 1985.

BIBLIOGRAPHY AND INDEX

The terms included in the book are listed in alphabetical order, followed by the page number on which their story starts (in parens), and the earliest citation for the term.

- A -

A Game of Inches (88): 'Clubs Fete Three Alton Grid Squads,' *Alton Evening Telegraph (IL)*, December 6, 1935.

Aerial Circus (94): 'Auburn Tigers Beaten By Rival's Air Attack,' *Birmingham News (AL)*, November 17, 1918.

All America (53): 'College News, *Salt Lake Tribune*, December 21, 1891.

Alligator Arms (161): 'Programming Gives Fans Restful Sunday, *Pittsburgh Post-Gazette*, October 10, 1983.

Armchair Quarterback (126): 'St. Thomas, Toronto Varsity Capture Rugby Titles,' *Windsor Star*, December 12, 1932.

Assistant Coach (17): 'Shooting Affray Follows The Game,' *Salt Lake Herald*, December 1, 1894.

Audible (148): Hyland, Dick, 'Van Brocklin, Brown Control West Destiny,' *Los Angeles Times*, January 12, 1956.

Away Game (52): 'Temple Lists 5 Owl Grid Frays,' *Tacoma Daily Ledger*, August 6, 1931.

- B -

Back or Sideline Judge (142): Sell, Jack, 'Sports Slants,' *Pittsburgh Press-Gazette*, June 17, 1947.

Back Shoulder Throw (206): Briggeman, Kim, 'A Victory To Savor,' *Missoulian (Missoula)*, September 9, 1996.

Ball Control Offense (150): McMullen, Lorin, 'Outlook Brightens for SEC Elevens, *Fort Worth Star-Telegram*, January 3, 1953.

Basic Fundamentals (95): 'Yale Star Here With U. Juniors,' *Tacoma Times*, October 23, 1915.

Blind Side or Blindside (88): 'Harvard Better Team Than Tigers,' Philadelphia Inquirer, November 9, 1915.

Blitz (139): ''Red Dogging' Is Old Grid Defense Play,' *Asbury Park Press*, November 18, 1958.

Blocking (7): 'College Teams At Football,' *New York Tribune*, November 4, 1883.

Blocking Machine (57): 'Movie Man Snaps Players In Action,' *South Bend News-Times*, September 19, 1914.

Blocking Sled (57): 'Varsity and Freshman Teams Scrimmage With New Plays Given Them,' *News-Democrat-Messenger (Bowling Green, KY)*, September 19, 1929.

Blocking Zone (199): Deitch, Scott E. (Ed.). 2000 NCAA Football Rules and Interpretations. Indianapolis: National Collegiate Athletic Association. 2000.

Bomb (104): 'Peabody Upsets Central Hi With Long Aerial Bomb,' *Tennessean (Nashville)*, November 28, 1929.

Booster (60): 'The Ottawa Football Booster,' *Ottawa Citizen*, October 31, 1898.

Bootleg (102): Wright, Theon, 'Brawn and Bulk Decide Battle of Year,' *Oakland Tribune*, November 20, 1927.

Boundary Corner (195): Sullivan, Mike, 'If 'Rampaging Heard' Plays It Smart, Speed Will Be Secondary at U of L,' *Courier-Journal (Louisville)*, September 9, 1976.

Bowl Game (128): Parker, Al, 'The Lookout,' *Wichita Falls Times*, November 28, 1935.

Bowl Season (128): 'Crystal Gazer Picks Stanford And West Teams, *Minneapolis Star*, December 31, 1934.

Box Office (22): 'Football and Baseball,' *Macon Telegraph (GA)*, November 8, 1893.

Box Seat (22): 'Cornell Wins The Game, *Chicago Tribune*, November 28, 1890.

Broken Field Runner (35): 'Sanford The Thing,' *Philadelphia Inquirer*, November 19, 1899.

Broken Play (35): 'Football In The Mud,' *St. Joseph News-Press (MO)*, November 3, 1922.

Bubble Screen (201): Kubat, Tom, "Bubble Screens Add Up To Dicken's Best Passing Day,' *Journal and Courier (Lafayette, IN)*, September 14, 1997.

Bull Rush (196): "Schmidt's The Difference' – Gordy,' *Detroit Free Press*, September 18, 1967.

Bunch Formation (201): 'Scouting Report,' *Democrat and Chronicle (Rochester, NY)*, January 26, 1992.

Button Hook (114): 'Football Review Given Spartans, *Lansing State Journal*, September 18, 1936.

- C -

Center/Centre (13): 'College Sport,' *New York Herald*, November 4, 1877. | 'Football,' *New York Daily Herald*, December 1, 1876.

Center Judge (190): Galaviz, Anthony, 'Fresno Referees Earn Spotlight, *Fresno Bee*, January 12, 2015

Chains (49): 'Football Chat,' *Evening World (New York)*, November 6, 1894.

Chain Gang (49): 'Lettermen To Be Announced At Grid Dinner,' *Pittsburgh Press*, November 30, 1921.

Chalk Talk (58): 'Town and County,' *Pittsfield Sun (MA)*, August 18, 1998.

Charging Machine (57): 'Secrecy At Cornell,' *Buffalo News*, November 21, 1900.

Checkerboard Field (60): 'Football Rules Favor Open Play,' *Chicago Tribune*, June 9, 1903.

Cheap Shot (172): McKinney, Jack, 'Inferiority Talk Gave Eagles Real Complex,' *Philadelphia Daily News*, October 1, 1960.

Cheap Shot Artist (172): 'Conerly Calls Bednarik Cheap-Shot Artist For Flattening Frank Gifford,' *Herald News (Passaic, NJ)*, November 21, 1960.

Cheerleader (25): 'Tigers Are In Good Shape,' *Times (Philadelphia)*, November 17, 1897.

Chin Strap (43): Frederick Loeser & Co, Line Up For Football,' *Brooklyn Daily Eagle*, October 7, 1904.

Chop Block (178): 'Quick Thrusts Give Fremont Impressive Win Over Redmen,' *News-Messenger (Fremont, OH)*, September 16, 1939.

Cleat (25): 'Football Costumes,' *San Francisco Chronicle*, January 26, 1890.

Clipping (107): 'No Drastic Changes In Football Rules This Season,' *Harrisburg Telegraph*, March 17, 1917.

Close Line Play (199): 'Stir Over Reid's Talk,' *Herald and Review (Decatur)*, November 11, 1905.

Clothesline Tackle (136): Nason, Jerry, 'Eagles Topple Boston Yanks In Debut, 28-7,' *Boston Globe*, September 27, 1944.

Coach (17): "The Sporting World, *Buffalo Morning Express and Illustrated*, October 7, 1889.

Coffin Corner Kick (91): Reed, Herbert, 'Opponents Endangered by Kick Into "Coffin" Corner,' *Herald and Review (Decatur, IL)*, October 5, 1919.

Combine, The (130): Byrod, Fred, '4 Dip Into One Pool for New Players,' *Philadelphia Inquirer*, September 9, 1965.

- D -

Draw Play (144): UPI, Calvin, Roy, 'Rice Gridders Had Things All Figured Out,' *Tribune (Scranton, PA),* January 3, 1950.

Dropback (133): Associated Press, 'Georgia Buries Tech, 34-0,' *Austin American,* November 30, 1941.

Dropback Passer (133): Bisher, Furman, 'Last Of The Campus Tycoons,' *Atlanta Constitution,* January 1, 1958.

Dropback Quarterback (133): Cullum, Dick, 'Cullum's Column,' *Star Tribune (Minneapolis),* July 14, 1964.

Drop Kick (12): 'Football,' *Brooklyn Union,* November 16, 1869.

Dual-Threat Quarterback (174): 'W. U. Faces Tough Humboldt,' *Capital Journal (Salem, OR),* September 30, 1961.

Dump (176): 'Action A-Plenty As Bobcats Win,' *Knoxville News-Sentinel,* November 4, 1932.

- E -

Edge Rusher (203): 'Rainbow Notes,' *Honolulu Star-Bulletin,* September 23, 1985.

Empty Formation (169): 'What To Watch,' *News Tribune (Tacoma),* November 17, 1991.

End (13): 'Yale's Great Day,' *Buffalo Morning Express,* November 25, 1887.

End Around (36): 'Cornell 0, Williams 0!,' *Buffalo Sunday Morning News,* November 15, 1896.

End Line (79): Camp, Walter, 'Camp Explains Football Rules,' *Pittsburgh Daily Post,* September 1, 1912.

End Zone (79): Camp, Walter, 'Camp Explains Football Rules,' *Pittsburgh Daily Post,* September 1, 1912.

- F -

Face Mask (40): 'Overman Wheel Co. Ad,' *Tulare Advance-Register,* July 31, 1897.

Facemasking (40): 'St. John's Closes Grid Campaign With 6-0 Win Over Franklin,' *Concord Monitor (VT),* November 13, 1962.

Fade Route (192): Roe, Joe, 'Packer Emotions Vary On Tie,' *Star Tribune (Minneapolis),* November 27, 1978.

Fair Catch (25): 'A Contest At Foot-Ball,' *New York Times,* December 15, 1878.

False Start (64): 'Crescents Win Again,' *Brooklyn Daily Eagle,* December 7, 1890.

Father of American Football (24): 'The Yale-Princeton Game, *Sun (New York),* November 27, 1886.

Field Corner (195): Florence, Mal, 'It's A Bit Like Father And Son...,' *Los Angeles Times,* September 1, 1985.

Field General (31): 'Makeup Of The S.U.I. Team,' *Omaha Daily Bee,* October 29, 1894.

Field Goal (12): 'Stalwart Kickers,' *Philadelphia Times,* November 11, 1883.

Field Judge (73): 'Two Changes Made,' *Boston Globe,* May 19, 1907.

First Half (26): 'Football,' *New York Daily Herald,* October 27, 1878.

First Quarter (95): 'New Football Rules Not Popular With College Coaches,' *Chattanooga News,* September 14, 1910.

First String (45): 'Secret Practice,' *Boston Globe,* May 13, 1900.

Five-Step Drop (187): Forbes, Gordon, 'Eagles Are Paying Dearly For Practice Lost In Strike,' *Philadelphia Inquirer,* November 19, 1974.

Flak Jacket (190): Sewell, Dick, 'Oiler Air Attack Beas Dolphins, 17-9,' *Montana Standard (Butte),* December 25, 1978.

Flag Route (103): 'Harvard Passes Produce Scores Against Old Eli,' *St. Louis Star and Times*, November 25, 1933.

Flanker (83): 'Hank Casserly Says:,' *Capital Times (Madison, WI)*, November 8, 1928.

Flat Pass (87): 'Nerve-Racking Forward Pass,' *Philadelphia Inquirer*, September 24, 1916.

Flea Flicker (84): Eckersall, Walter, "Prep Champions Of West Humble St. John's By 17-0, *Chicago Tribune*, December 3, 1911.

Flex Tight End (193): Newman, Chuck, 'After The Fall: Maryland, O'Hara Wait For Villanova,' *Philadelphia Inquirer*, September 7, 1971.

Flood Pattern (131): Hollingberry, Gabe, 'Grid-Ironies,' *Public Opinion (Chambersburg, PA)*, October 21, 1942.

Flying Wedge (16): 'Yale Wins From Harvard,' *San Francisco Examiner*, November 20, 1892.

Football (1): 'Football,' *Brooklyn Union*, November 16, 1869.

Football Sweater (20): 'Trinity College Notes,' *Hartford Courant*, March 2, 1996.

Forward Pass (65): 'College Football,' *Philadelphia Inquirer*, November 17, 1887.

Forward Progress (9): 'Foot-Ball Made Clear,' *Philadelphia Times*, November 12, 1893.

Four-Down Territory (164): Smith, Red, 'Views of Sport,' *San Bernardino County Sun*, June 27, 1958.

Fourth Quarter (95): 'New Football Rules Not Popular With College Coaches,' *Chattanooga News*, September 14, 1910.

Free Blocking Zone (199): Thomas, Jim, 'Prep-JC Beat,' *Daily Breeze (Torrance, CA)*, January 11, 1981.

Free Safety (160): Sainsbury, Ed, 'Bears Need Offense To Cash In On Flag,' *Courier Post (Camden, NJ)*, September 10, 1958.

Full House T (177): McLeod, George, 'Wildcats Ponder Hard-To-Shatter Poke Interference,' *Tucson Citizen*, November 2, 1961.

Fullback (13): 'Students As Kickers, *New York Times*, October 17, 1880.

Fumble (8): 'Foot-Ball Between Princeton and Lafayette, *Philadelphia Times*, October 23, 1883.

- G -

Gadget Play (168): 'Gillman Expects Several 'Gadget' Plays This Year,' *Daily Independent Journal (San Rafael)*, August 13, 1959.

Game Clock (110): Dana, Herb, 'When To Substitute Big Gridiron Puzzle,' *San Francisco Examiner*, September 13, 1932.

Gang Tackle (108): Brannon, Earl W., 'Cornhuskers Crush Kansas In Decisive, Hard-Fought Battle,' *Lincoln Star (NE)*, November 16, 1913.

Gap Responsibility (159): Thomy, Al, 'Pro Defenses Changing To Meet Threat,' *Atlanta Constitution*, August 28, 1968.

Get Back Coach (199): Towle, Mike, 'On The Range,' *Fort Worth Star-Telegram*, November 27, 1986.

Goal (4): 'Football,' *Brooklyn Union*, November 16, 1869.

Goal from Field (12): 'Sporting Matters,' *Boston Globe*, November 28, 1881.

Goal Line (4): 'Football,' *Brooklyn Union*, November 16, 1869.

Goal Line Stand (73): 'Harvard Barely Tied Dartmouth,' *Washington Times*, November 19, 1905.

Goal Posts (4): 'Football,' *Brooklyn Union*, November 16, 1869.

G.O.A.T. (Greatest of All Time) (204): Smith, Michael, 'There Must Be A Backup Plan,' *Boston Globe*, September 28, 2001.

- H -

- I -

Icing the Kicker (197): Turnbull, Buck, 'Hawkeyes Survive Purdue Scare, 27-24,' *Des Moines Register*, October 17, 1985.

In The Grasp (9): 'Football Reformers Yield to Walter Camp,' *Brooklyn Daily Eagle*, February 11, 1906.

Inbound Lines (121): 'N.D. High Schools Will Play Under Interscholastic Rules,' *Bismarck Tribune*, September 14, 1934.

Incomplete Pass (66): 'Camp Makes Rules Clear,' *Boston Globe*, October 5, 1907.

Incompletion (66): Rice, Grantland, 'Sportville Echoes,' *Tennessean (Nashville)*, December 24, 1907.

Injured Reserve List (138): 'Bulldogs Cut Down To 28 Players For League Opener Wed. Night,' *Morning Call (Allentown, PA)*, September 30, 1947.

Inline Tight End (193): 'Key Matchups,' *Austin American-Statesman*, January 25, 1987.

Instant Replay (177): Jackaubowsky, Jack. 'Between the Lines,' *Redwood City Tribune (CA)*, October 1, 1964.

Interception (67): 'They May Tie Us, But Can't Beat Us,' *Philadelphia Inquirer*, October 29, 1899.

- J -

Jet Motion (200): 'Buena's & Delsea's Bread 'N' Butter Plays,' *Daily Journal (Vineland, NJ)*, December 5, 2002.

Jet Sweep (200): Herzberg, Mike, 'Cotter Blanks Viroqua For Fourth Football Win,' *Winona Daily News (MN)*, September 23, 1980.

- K -

Kicking Shoe (60): 'School Teams Practice,' *Pittsburgh Weekly Gazette*, November 8, 1904.

- L -

Late Hit (172): Maysel, Lou, 'Top O' Morn,' *Austin American*, November 21, 1961.

Lateral or Lateral Pass (87): 'Yale Vanquished By Minor College,' *Hartford Courant*, October 25, 1914.

Laundry on the Field (139): 'Laundry On The Field – Yellow On The Green,' *Malvern Leader (IA)*, November 11, 1976.

Letter Jacket (20): 'Sports Jackets Are Presented Tigers Monday,' *Waxahachie Daily Light (TX)*, February 6, 1933.

Letter Sweater (20): 'The Bethany Record,' *Lindsborg Record (KS)*, December 18, 1903.

Line Judge (177): Meyer, Joe, 'Sideline On Sports,' *Edwardsville Intelligencer (IL)*, April 14, 1965.

Line of Scrimmage (61): 'Vital Change,' *Boston Globe*, September 17, 1895.

Linebacker (46): 'Review Of The Games,' *Buffalo Courier*, October 22, 1895.

Lockney Lines (121): 'Lockney's 'Lines' Get More Favorable Comments; Big Ten May Adopt Unique Marking System,' *Waukesha Freeman*, October 30, 1954.

Long Snapping (176): Busey, Bob, 'The Breaks In K.U.-Oklahoma Game About Evenly Divided,' *Kansas City Times*, October 2, 1947.

- O -

Off Tackle (59): 'Holds Iowa Even,' *Inter Ocean (Chicago)*, November 30, 1900.
Offense (13): Tigers Worst Yale, *Chicago Tribune*, December 1, 1893.
Offensive Coordinator (161): 'Cornell Grid Staff Adds 2,' *Clarion-Ledger (Jackson, MS)*, May 24, 1962.
Offensive Line (13): 'The Thanksgiving Game,' *Omaha Daily Bee*, November 19, 1893.
Offensive Line Coach (102): 'Bach Will Meet Officials Today,' *Atlanta Constitution*, March 14, 1925.
Offside (7): 'College Kickers,' *Boston Globe*, November 12, 1883.
Onside (7): 'College Kickers,' *Boston Globe*, November 12, 1883.
One-Two Blocking (99): 'Rutledge, Storrs Are Outstanding in Lubbock Win, *Lubbock Morning Avalanche*, October 24, 1936.
Onside Kick (28): 'Harvard's Easy Win,' *Chicago Tribune*, December 1, 1893.
Option Play (141): Ledden, Jack, 'Irish Opponents Split As Drake Loses,' *South Bend Tribune*, October 4, 1937.
Orbit Motion (206): 'Concentrating Makes Their Game,' *News and Observer (Raleigh)*, October 6, 1999.
Oskie (108): ''Oskie Wow Wow!' Must Save Jackets,' *Atlanta Constitution*, October 10, 1950.
Out of Bounds (5): 'Foot Ball,' *Brooklyn Daily Eagle*, November 21, 1879.
Outside Linebacker (159): Hart, Weldon, 'Longhorns Near Top Shape for Supreme Bid Against Bitter Aggies,' *Austin American-Statesman*, November 24, 1942.

- P -

Pancake Block (179): 'Sypult Gets Second WVU Football Star,' *Beckley Post-Herald (WV)*, October 27, 1966.
Pass (65): 'Football,' *Brooklyn Union*, November 16, 1869.
Pass Pattern (130): Moore, Paul, 'Sports Notes,' *Corsicana Daily*, September 1, 1939.
Pass Receiving (66): 'Not Much Thanksgiving,' *Daily Mail (Wellington, KS)*, November 29, 1907.
Pass Reception (66): 'Harvard Team To Invade West,' *El Paso Herald*, December 4, 1919.
Pass Route (130): Griffith, Jim, 'Lanier Poets Face Tough Scrimmages,' *Macon Telegraph (GA)*, October 18, 1943.
Passing Tree (170): McDonough, Will, 'Thumbnail Football, Parilli Gives Pass Routes Used By Ends and Flankers,' *Boston Globe*, October 28, 1962.
Penalty Flag (139): 'High Nudges Coaldale; Catholic Corks Shenandoah,' *Mount Carmel Item (PA)*, October 29, 1945.
Personnel Grouping or Package (198): Dodd, Mike, 'Bengals Mix and Match Linebackers,' *Cincinnati Enquirer*, November 8, 1985.
Physicality (202): Waters, Bill, 'On Wildcats Pre-Iowa Docket: A Week Of Hard Work, *Arizona Daily Star*, September 29, 1969.
Physically Unable to Perform (PUP) List (138): Forbes, Dick, 'Ballou Details QB Arm Record,' *Cincinnati Enquirer*, August 15, 1970.
Pick (67): Anderson, Dave, 'Rookies In The Super Bowl Spotlight,' *Press Democrat (Santa Rosa, CA)*, January 22, 1982.
Pick Six (67): Moore, Brad, 'What Went Wrong,' *Albuquerque Tribune*, November 18, 2002.
Picked Off (67): 'St. Edward's Defeats West Texas Military,' *Austin American-Statesman*, November 6, 1909.

Pigskin (3): 'Yale's Easy Victory,' *New York Times*, November 3, 1886.

Place Kick (12): 'How to Play Football,' *St. Louis Post-Dispatch*, November 25, 1888.

Placer (12): 'How to Play Football,' *St. Louis Post-Dispatch*, November 25, 1888.

Play-Action Pass (133): McKinney, Jack, 'Ah Yes, Packers In A Class All Their Own,' *Philadelphia Daily News*, November 12, 1962.

Play Clock (110): 'Sub Rule Needs Change – Phelan,' *Eugene Guard*, November 11, 1947,

Playbook (147): 'UW's Bruhn Had Bad Moment Before Finding Missing Play Book,' *Green Bay Gazette*, December 18, 1952.

Pocket Protection (143): 'Cleveland Captures Title Clash, 31 to 28,' *Oakland Tribune*, November 29, 1948.

Point of Attack (32): 'Football And War,' *Pittsburgh Dispatch*, November 29, 1991.

Pooch Kick (189): 'Porker Linemen Will Miss Opener,' *Shreveport Journal*, September 13, 1963.

Post Route (181): Meyers, Charlie, 'Gators Bomb Vikings, 35-0,' *Lake Charles American Press (LA)*, October 17, 1964.

Press Box (22): 'Yale 12 Princeton 0,' *Evening World (New York)*, November 24, 1992.

Prevent Defense (160): Associated Press, 'Lions Escape USC Comeback,' *Daily News (Huntingdon, PA)*, December 9, 1955.

Primary Defense (39): 'Coaches Finding The Weak Places,' *Boston Globe*, October 22, 1999.

Progression Read (194): Twitty, Mike, 'Raider Backup QB Wilson 'Excited About Season'',' *Daily Herald (Provo)*, July 30, 1981.

Punt (12): 'Football,' *New York Daily Herald*, December 18, 1876.

- Q -

Quarterback (13): 'Football,' *Leeds Mercury (UK)*, February 22, 1876.

Quarterback Sneak (71): 'Tigers Claw Extracted,' *Chattanooga Daily Times*, November 18, 1917.

Quick Kick (26): 'New York, 24; Staten Island, 0,.' *New York Times*, November 17, 1889.

- R -

Read Option (203): Spencer, Bill, 'Newton's Tillman Rising Star At QB,' *Clarion Ledger (MS)*, September 3, 1998.

Reading Defenses (148): Hall, Flem, 'The Sport Tide,' *Fort Worth Star-Telegram*, October 5, 1954.

Red Zone (185): Associated Press, Nelson, John, Broadcast Big Hit, From Ads To Guys In Booth,' *Indiana Gazette (PA)*, June 23, 1978.

Receiver (66): 'P. A. C. Players Leave For The Woods,' *Pittsburgh Daily Post*, November 7, 1898.

Receiving Yardage (66): 'Governali's Passes Click,' *Central New Jersey Home News (New Brunswick)*, November 5, 1942.

Red Dog (139): 'Mercury Fall, Odds Climb for Rams-Bears Crucial Tilt,' *Los Angeles Times*, November 25, 1950.

Redshirt (117): 'Putting on Speed for Cornell Game,' *Philadelphia Inquirer*, November 28, 1917.

Redshirting (117): Hewitt, Purser, 'Sports,' *Clarion-Ledger (Jackson, MS)*, September 11, 1939.

Referee (7): 'Tufts Beats Bates At Football,' *Portland Daily Press*, November 8, 1875.

Reverse (36): 'Yale, 24; Princeton, 0,' *New York Times*, December 2, 1894.

Roughing (28): 'Football Slugging,' *Brooklyn Citizen*, November 1, 1891.

Rouge (12): 'Football,' *Leeds Mercury (UK)*, February 22, 1876.

Rugby (1): 'Rugby School,' *Burlington Weekly Free Press*, March 19, 1869.

Run Out The Clock (136): 'Kiser Beats Chaminade, 8-6, Co-Shares Big Six Crown,' *Dayton Herald*, November 22, 1942.

Run-Pass Option (RPO) (204): Bell, Gregg, 'Raiders Will Stay With Gannon,' *Sacramento Bee*, September 24, 2003.

Running Back (13): 'Crimson Strong,' *Boston Post*, October 15, 1893.

- S -

Sack (176): 'Rams Do It With Offense... And Defense, Too,' *Los Angeles Times*, October 20, 1969.

Safety (score) (12): 'The Sporting World,' *Boston Globe*, December 9, 1877.

Safety (position) (46): 'Central Won By Score of 17-0,' *Leavenworth Times*, October 5, 1902.

Safety Blitz (172): 'Randle Trails Leader Mithcell By One In N.F.L. Pass Catching,' *St. Louis Post-Dispatch*, November 14, 1962.

Safety Touchdown (12): 'Football,' *Hartford Courant*, December 10, 1877.

Sam Linebacker (160): McGrotha, Bill, 'With Little Bit Of Luck – Watch Out For Defense,' *Tallahassee Democrat*, April 29, 1971.

Scrambling Quarterback (174): Thomy, Al, 'It Was A T(errific)-Day For Auer,' *Atlanta Constitution*, April 30, 1962.

Screen Pass (68): 'Two Aspects of Forward Pass,' *Fairmont West Virginian*, November 11, 1915.

Scrimmage (119): 'Foot-Ball Match – Germantown Cricket,' *Philadelphia Inquirer*, November 18, 1869.

Scoop-and-Score (8): 'James Feels At Home On The Ground,' *Tampa Bay Times*, November 4, 1996.

Scout Team (117): 'Huskers Take Last Work-Out For Sooners,' *McCook Daily Gazette*, November 23, 1939.

Scrimmage Vest (119): 'Call For Bids,' *Carlsbad Current-Argus (NM)*, January 7, 1945.

Scrub (45): 'Football At Princeton,' *New York Times*, October 2, 1884.

Scrummage (6): 'Foot Ball,' *St. Louis Globe-Democrat*, March 11, 1876.

Seam Route (192): Inman, Hank, 'Sooners' Next Foe 'Basically' Sound,' *Daily Oklahoman (Oklahoma City)*, September 23, 1974.

Second Guesser (126): 'Business Cards,' *Freeman's Journal (Dublin, IR)*, September 21, 1888. | 'Winning Guesses,' *Minneapolis Journal*, November 2, 1903.

Second Half (26): 'Football,' *New York Daily Herald*, October 27, 1878.

Second Quarter (95): 'New Football Rules Not Popular With College Coaches,' *Chattanooga News*, September 14, 1910.

Secondary Defense (39): 'Quackers' Fine Play,' *Inter Ocean (Chicago)*, November 20, 1898.

Seven-Step Drop (187): Forbes, Gordon, 'Eagles Are Paying Dearly For Practice Lost In Strike,' *Philadelphia Inquirer*, November 19, 1974.

Shift (32): 'That New Football Play,' *Sun (New York)*, December 3, 1899.

Shifted Formation (32): Brooke, George H. 'Coach Brooke Discusses New Game's Shifting Attack,' *Washington Post*, November 18, 1906.

Shock Troops (90): Fullerton, Hugh, 'Fullerton's Column,' *Yonkers Herald*, November 4, 1921.

Shoestring Tackle (75): 'High School Eleven Showing Up Stronger,' *Anaconda Standard*, October 10, 1906.

Shotgun (169): 'Secret Practice,' *Port Angeles Evening News (WA)*, November 9, 1960,

Shoulder Pads (42): 'Princeton's Good Showing,' *Philadelphia Inquirer*, November 21, 1895.

Time Of Possession (188): Herman, Jeff, 'Spartans Outlast Broncs,' *Missoulian (Missoula)*, September 23, 1972.

Timing Route (187): Anderson, Andy, 'Cowboy Corner,' *Odessa American*, October 16, 1971.

Touchback (12): 'Work Of The Kickers,' *Boston Globe*, November 2, 1884.

Touchdown (9): 'International Football Match,' *Burlington Free Press*, October 26, 1874

Touch Line (5): 'University Notes,' Daily Illini, December 1, 1878.

Trainer (19): 'Yale Notes,' *Morning Journal-Courier (New Haven)*, October 23, 1886.

Training Camp (46): 'A Kick Among The Kickers,' *Post-Crescent (Appleton, WI)*, August 19, 1899.

Training Table (26): 'College Football,' *Sun (New York)*, December 12, 1889.

Trap Block (70): 'The Dakotas At Football,' *Argus-Leader (Sioux Falls, SD)*, November 12, 1908.

Trenches (86): Napier, Jr., Charles R., 'Manual Outlook Best, Says Ligda,' *Los Angeles Evening Express*, September 12, 1916.

Trick Play (36): 'Whitewashed,' *San Francisco Call*, March 15, 1891.

Trickeration (202): Koch, Bill, 'Kelly Pulls Off 'Trickeration',' *Cincinnati Enquirer*, November 4, 2007.

Triple Option (180): Nichols, Ed, 'Sport Shorts,' *Daily Times (Salisbury, MD)*, October 16, 1953.

Turf Toe (180): 'Saint Waiting Again,' *Northwest Arkansas Times (Fayetteville)*, September 6, 1972.

Two-Gap Responsibility (159): 'Hutchinson Can Play In The Middle,' *Tampa Tribune*, October 27, 1976.

Two-Minute Drill (136): 'Iowa State Defenses T Offense,' *Ames Daily Tribune*, September 2, 1960.

Two-Minute Warning (136): 'Tacoma High Defeats Old Rival On Gridiron,' *Tacoma Daily Ledger*, October 17, 1909.

Two-On-One Blocking (99): 'Big Change In Utah Grid Lines Seen In Future,' *Deseret News (Salt Lake City)*, June 18, 1928.

Two-Platoon (135): 'Eagles To Work In Two Platoons, So Leahy Says,' *Boston Globe*, November 7, 1940.

- U -

Umpire (7): 'Foot-Ball Match – Germantown Cricket,' *Philadelphia Inquirer*, November 18, 1869.

Unbalanced Formation (32): 'Oddities of Football,' *Kenosha News*, December 20, 1899.

Uncompleted (66): Camp, Walter (Ed.). *Spalding's Official Foot Ball Rules*. New York: American Sports Publishing. 1907.

Under Center (82): 'Yale's Great Day,' *Buffalo Morning Express*, November 25, 1887.

Uprights (4): 'Blame The Umpire,' *Inter Ocean (Chicago)*, October 30, 1892.

- V -

Varsity (1): 'Harvard's Improved Game,' *New York Times*, November 5, 1894.

Varsity Sweater (20): 'The Gold Foot-Balls,' *Hartford Courant*, February 2, 1893.

Veer: (180): Johnson, Bob, 'My Nickel's Worth,' *Spokane Chronicle*, August 30, 1967.

- W -

Walk-On (117): Cornelius, Lew, 'Scorebook,' *Capital Times (Madison, WI)*, December 12, 1964.

Watch Charm (20): 'Gold and Silver Football Charms,' *Decatur Daily Review*, November 21, 1921.

Weak Side (32): 'Brooke, George E., Coach Brookes Explains New System Of Attack, *Washington Post*, October 28, 1906.

Wedge (16): 'College Football Games' *New York Times*, October 27, 1889.

Wheel Route (200): Kensler, Tom, 'This Win Was Matter Of Time For Cowboys,' *Daily Oklahoman (Oklahoma City)*, November 1, 1982.

Wideout (157): Amdur, Neil, 'Tragedy Follows Tennessee's Resurgence As Power,' *Miami Herald*, September 7, 1966.

Wide Receiver (83): 'Gerstmeyer Gridders Capture City Grid Championship,' *Terre Haute Tribune*, November 12, 1950.

Will Linebacker (160): McGrotha, Bill, 'With Little Bit Of Luck – Watch Out For Defense,' *Tallahassee Democrat*, April 29, 1971.

Wind Sprints (75): 'How Things Look Three Days Before Big Gridiron Battle,' *Grand Forks Herald*, October 28, 1908.

Wishbone (180): Lutz, Michael, '2nd Spectacular On The Way,' *Corpus Christi Times*, September 27/, 1968.

- X -

X (157): Panella, Bob, 'Sports Row,' *Los Angeles Evening Citizen News*, August 5, 1957.

X's and O's (105): 'Hank Casserly Says…', *Capitol Times (Madison, WI)*, December 9, 1927.

- Y -

Y (157): Panella, Bob, 'Sports Row,' *Los Angeles Evening Citizen News*, August 5, 1957.

Yard Line (6): 'Hot Work On A Cool Day,' *New York Times*, November 14, 1880.

Yard-Line Extensions (121): Has not appeared in a newspaper as of November 7, 2022.

Yards After Catch (YAC) (187): 'Bengals Drawing Defenses For Rice,' *Cincinnati Enquirer*, December 7, 1990.

Yellow Laundry (139): Haslam, Greg, 'Rebels Come Out On Top Of 37-14 Decision Over Utah JV,' *Daily Spectrum (St. George, UT)*, November 5, 1978.

- Z -

Z (157): Panella, Bob, 'Sports Row,' *Los Angeles Evening Citizen News*, August 5, 1957.

Zone Blocking (186): 'New Indiana Grid Coach To Install Side-Saddle T,' *Battle Creek Enquirer*, January 27, 1957.

Zone Defense (97): Casey, Eddie, 'The Forward Pass Defense,' *Charlotte News*, October 28, 1920.

Zone Read (203): Halliburton, Susan, 'Texas Offense In Young's Hands,' *Austin American-Statesman*, October 3, 2003.

ILLUSTRATIONS

Certain illustrations are from the following books.

Camp, Walter. *Spalding's 1899 Official Foot Ball Guide*. New York: American Sports Publishing New York, 1899.

Camp, Walter (Ed.). *Spalding's Official Foot Ball Guide for 1906*. New York: American Sports Publishing, 1906.

Camp, Walter (Ed.). *Spalding's Official Foot Ball Rules*. New York: American Sports Publishing, 1907.

Camp, Walter (Ed.). *Spalding's Official Foot Ball Guide for 1908*. New York: American Sports Publishing, 1908.

Camp, Walter (Ed.). *1917 Official Foot Ball Rules*. New York: American Sports Publishing, 1917.

Redding, Rogers (Ed.). *2009-2010 NCAA Football Rules and Interpretations*. Indianapolis: National Collegiate Athletic Association, 2009.

Bible, Dana X. Championship Football: A Guide for Player, Coach, Fan. New York: Prentice-Hall, 1947.

Camp, Walter and Lorin F. Deland. *Football*. Houghton, Mifflin, Boston, 1896.

Daly, Charles D. *American Football*. New York: Harper & Brothers. 1921.

Davis, Parke H. *Football: The American Intercollegiate Game.* New York: Charles Scribner's Sons, 1911.

Edwards, William H. *Football Days: Memories of the Game and of the Men Behind the Ball.* New York: Moffat, Yard and Company, 1916.

Faurot, Don. *Football: Secrets of the "Split T" Formation.* New York: Prentice-Hall, 1950.

Haughton, Percy D. *Football and How to Watch It.* Boston, Marshall Jones, 1922.

Oakes, Bernard F. *Football Line Play (Revised).* New York: A.S. Barnes, 1948.

Official Football Rules of the National Collegiate Athletic Association. New York: National Collegiate Athletic Bureau, 1957.

Presbrey, Frank and Frank Hugh Moffat (Eds.). *Athletics at Princeton, A History.* New York: Graduate Advisory Committee, 1901.

Reed, Herbert. *Football for Public and Player.* New York, Frederick A. Stokes, 1913.

Stagg, A. Alonzo and Henry L. Williams. *Scientific and Practical Treatise on American Football for Schools and Colleges.* Hartford: Case, Lockwood & Brained, 1893.

Warner, Glenn. *A Course in Football for Players and Coaches.* Carlisle, PA, 1912.

Zuppke, Robert C. *Football, Techniques and Tactics.* Champaign, IL: Bailey & Himes, 1924.

ALSO BY TIMOTHY P. BROWN

Fields of Friendly Strife: The Doughboys and Sailors of the WWI Rose Bowls

How Football Became Football: 150 Years of the Game's Evolution

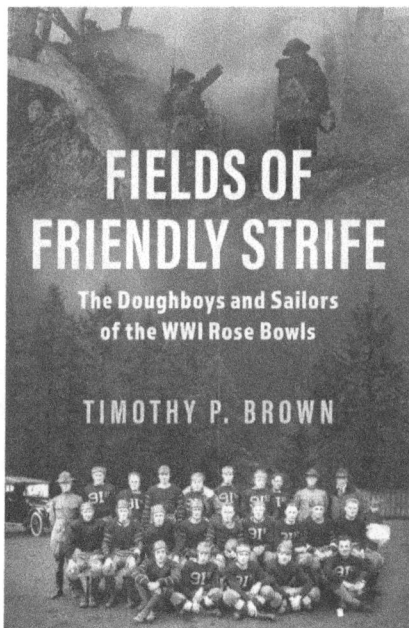

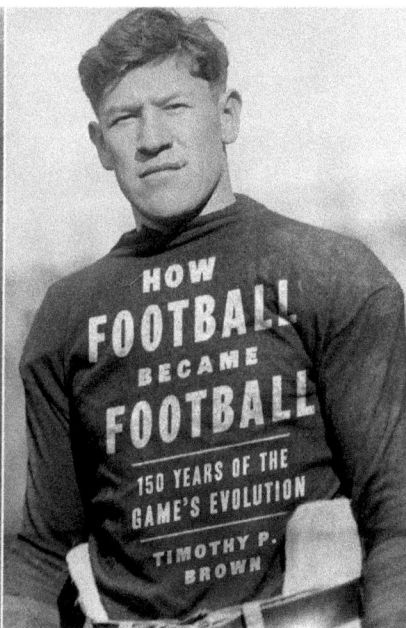

1.0